BASEBALL
Faith

ROB MAADDI

BASEBALL *Faith*

52 MLB Stars Reflect on Their Faith

SHILOH RUN ▲ PRESS

An Imprint of Barbour Publishing, Inc.

Published by Shiloh Run Press, an imprint of Barbour Publishing, Inc., P.O. Box 719, Uhrichsville, Ohio 44683, www.shilohrunpress.com.

Our mission is to publish and distribute inspirational products offering exceptional value and biblical encouragement to the masses.

ecpa Member of the
Evangelical Christian
Publishers Association

Printed in China.

DEDICATION

For Jesus Christ, thank You for the ultimate sacrifice, taking that cross and guiding me every minute of my life. For my twin daughters, Alexia and Melina, you will always be daddy's little girls, and I love you more than words can adequately describe. For my loving wife, Remy, thank you for your support, encouragement, and unconditional love. For my parents, Issa and Hayat, thank you for everything. Special thanks to Diego Ettedgui and Gethin Coolbaugh for all your help on this project.

"The King will reply, 'Truly I tell you, whatever you did for one of the least of these brothers and sisters of mine, you did for me.'"
MATTHEW 25:40

They hit prodigious home runs. They reach triple digits on the radar gun. They make acrobatic catches.

Some are Hall of Famers. Some are perennial All-Stars. Some are just average ballplayers living the dream in the major leagues.

They compete hard on the field and play to win. In real life, they're all on the same team. They're a brotherhood, a fraternity, a group of men who share a passion for Christ.

Superior talent and elite skills make them seem larger than life. However, they're just like you and me. They have ups and downs, good days and bad days. They sometimes have struggles. They often have to overcome adversity.

Through life's smooth and rough moments, they rely on God. There's no greater teammate or better coach than the Lord.

Baseball Faith provides a unique and inside look at some of the greatest players in baseball history and guides you through their Christian journey.

CONTENTS

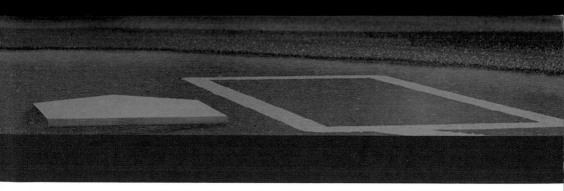

CHASE ANDERSON

For God did not send his Son into the world to condemn the world, but to save the world through him.

JOHN 3:17

You hear so much about John 3:16—"For God so loved the world that he gave his one and only Son, that whoever believes in him shall not perish but have eternal life"—and then you read this verse and realize the Lord didn't come to condemn us; He came to save us. People think there's a lot of hypocrisy in Christianity, and there may be some hypocrites, but Jesus didn't come here to be served but to serve and save us from this world because there's something bigger for us in heaven.

I grew up going to church here and there. I wasn't a strong Christian. But when my grandmother passed away in 2009, she left me her Bible, and some of the verses in there hit me hard. The biggest turning point for me came when my dad passed away in 2012, because we were very close. My parents divorced when I was twelve, and I lived with him. We were like peas and carrots. We did everything together—worked, played baseball. He lived vicariously through me. So when he passed away, it was a big turning point for me, and I rededicated my life as a Christian. I realized I need a Savior because I can't do this myself.

Chase Anderson

POSITION	Pitcher
HEIGHT	6 foot 1
WEIGHT	200 lbs
BATS	Right
THROWS	Right
NUMBER	57
BORN	November 30, 1987, in Wichita Falls, Texas
HIGH SCHOOL	Rider (Wichita Falls, Texas)
COLLEGE	Oklahoma
DRAFTED	By Arizona Diamondbacks in 9th round of the 2009 amateur draft
HONORS	All-State pitcher and shortstop as high school senior
TEAMS	Arizona Diamondbacks (2014–15); Milwaukee Brewers (2016–)

SEVENTH INNING STRETCH

Chase Anderson tossed three no-hitters as a high school senior.

Chase Anderson won his first five major league starts and finished 10th in voting for National League Rookie of the Year in 2014. After a solid sophomore season, Anderson was part of a five-player trade from Arizona to Milwaukee.

CAREER STATS

PITCHING				
Games	GS	W	L	CG
79	78	24	24	0
SHO	SV	ERA	IP	K
0	0	4.26	274	336

ANDREW BAILEY

Trust in the LORD with all your heart and lean not on your own understanding; in all your ways submit to him, and he will make your paths straight.

PROVERBS 3:5–6

I learned this verse early on in the minor leagues at baseball chapel. It stuck with me through all the ups and downs on and off the field. My daughter was born six weeks early with some medical issues. She has a mild case of cerebral palsy, and while she was in the hospital, I trusted in the Lord and knew that, whatever happened, things would be fine. Living by that verse keeps me focused on the ultimate goal. During that rough time, reading that verse at night while she was sleeping kept me on the right path.

We're all in our own place in our relationship with Christ. For me, it's been a rocky road at times. There are times in life when you fall off that path, but you jump back on, and at the end of the day, He's always there for you. He knows what you're going to be going through before you do, and there's always a way out of it, no matter what it is. I definitely encourage kids to find the Bible and start reading because it can change your life.

Andrew Bailey

POSITION	Pitcher
HEIGHT	6 foot 3
WEIGHT	240 lbs
BATS	Right
THROWS	Right
NUMBER	37
BORN	May 31, 1984, in Voorhees, New Jersey
HIGH SCHOOL	Paul VI (Haddonfield, New Jersey)
COLLEGE	Wagner College
DRAFTED	By Oakland A's in 6th round of the 2006 amateur draft
HONORS	2009 American League Rookie of the Year, two-time American League All-Star
TEAMS	Oakland A's (2009–11); Boston Red Sox (2012–13); New York Yankees (2015); Philadelphia Phillies (2016); Los Angeles Angels (2016)

Andrew Bailey has an ERA below 3.00 in every inning except the seventh, when it's 6.56.

Bailey quickly became Oakland's closer after breaking into the major leagues in 2009 and had an outstanding season. After saving 75 games for the A's in three seasons, he was traded to Boston and injuries began to derail his career; but Bailey finished the 2016 season back in his closer's role and was 6 for 6 in September.

CAREER STATS

PITCHING				
Games	GS	W	L	CG
261	0	14	14	0
SHO	SV	ERA	IP	K
0	95	3.16	270.1	274

DUSTY BAKER

*Do not lurk like a thief near the house of the righteous,
do not plunder their dwelling place; for though the
righteous fall seven times, they rise again, but
the wicked stumble when calamity strikes.*

Proverbs 24:15–16

This verse applied in my life when I was up and down, up and down. When you rise to the top, you have to keep the faith, especially when the Lord has delivered you more than once. I've been up and I've been down with seemingly no way out, and then the Lord delivered me again. And then it happened a couple more times. It's a hard way to go. I don't think of myself as a righteous man as it says, but our Lord has delivered me many times in my life because of the faith I was raised with. Sometimes I would wonder why He did so because I felt so undeserving, but that's how God is. My family started me out in the church at a very young age. If you were too sick to go to church that Sunday, you didn't go out to play, so I was the same way with my daughter and son.

The Lord has delivered me through many trials and tribulations and given me a sense of calmness that lets me know things will always work out, and that's what keeps me going no matter what. People always see the successes, but they don't see the failures in your life. They don't see the times when you were going broke, losing money, getting divorced, and thought you had hit rock bottom. The Lord gives you the sense of purpose that you have to have. There are many people out there who are faithless and feel a sense of hopelessness and despair. I'm here to tell them that if you persevere, the Lord will always come through and deliver you.

Dusty Baker

POSITION	Outfielder
HEIGHT	6 foot 2
WEIGHT	183 lbs
BATS	Right
THROWS	Right
NUMBER	12
BORN	June 15, 1949, in Riverside, California
HIGH SCHOOL	Del Campo HS (Fair Oaks, California), El Campo HS (Citrus Heights, California)
COLLEGE	American River College
DRAFTED	By Atlanta Braves in 26th round of the 1967 amateur draft
HONORS	Two-time All-Star, one-time Gold Glove Award winner, three-time Manager of the Year
TEAMS	As player—Atlanta Braves (1968–75); Los Angeles Dodgers (1976–83); San Francisco Giants (1984); Oakland A's (1985–86)
	As manager—San Francisco Giants (1993–2002); Chicago Cubs (2003–06); Cincinnati Reds (2008–13); Washington Nationals (2016–)

On April 8, 1974, Dusty Baker was on deck when Hank Aaron hit home run 715 to pass Babe Ruth in career home runs.

Dusty Baker was a hard-hitting slugger for 19 seasons in the majors, reaching the postseason four times and helping the Los Angeles Dodgers win the 1981 World Series. Baker followed up his success on the field with an excellent career in the dugout, winning more than 1,700 games as a manager over 20 seasons while leading four teams to the postseason.

CAREER STATS

BATTING			
Games	AVG	OBP	SLG
2,039	.278	.347	.432
Hits	HR	RBI	SB
1,981	242	1,013	137

LANCE BERKMAN

"I am the vine; you are the branches. If you remain in me and I in you, you will bear much fruit; apart from me you can do nothing."

JOHN 15:5

This is my favorite verse because many people often think being a "good person" is good enough. They think if the good you do outweighs the bad you do, then you're in good standing with God. This verse really stands out for me because anything we do that's good apart from the power and the name of Jesus Christ—not that it doesn't count—but from a spiritual standpoint, it's not edifying. It's not worth much. The only way we can truly have a purpose and an enriching life experience is to do all things in Christ and through the power of Christ. If we're only concerned with doing good works and we're doing that outside of the power of Christ, we end up getting the glory, and God deserves the glory. This verse illustrates that point perfectly.

Reading the Bible is how we feed ourselves spiritually. We eat to feed ourselves physically; but in order to be truly alive, we have to feed our spiritual lives, and that's accomplished by reading, studying, and meditating on God's Word.

If you practice what the Bible says, your life is better for it. Becoming a Christian doesn't eliminate all your problems, but if you pattern your life after Jesus, you will experience that spiritual life.

Lance Berkman

POSITION	Outfielder, first baseman
HEIGHT	6 foot 1
WEIGHT	220 lbs
BATTED	Both
THREW	Left
NUMBER	27
BORN	February 10, 1976, in Waco, Texas
HIGH SCHOOL	Canyon (New Braunfels, Texas)
COLLEGE	Rice University
DRAFTED	By Houston Astros in 1st round (16th overall) of the 1997 amateur draft
HONORS	Six-time All-Star, 2011 National League Comeback Player of the Year
TEAMS	Houston Astros (1999–2010); New York Yankees (2010); St. Louis Cardinals (2011–12); Texas Rangers (2013)

Berkman finished in the top 10 in voting for Most Valuable Player six times.

Lance Berkman was one of the best switch-hitting sluggers in major league history, ranking sixth in career home runs. He had six 30-homer seasons, including two with more than 40. He surpassed 100 runs batted six times and led the league once.

CAREER STATS

BATTING			
Games	AVG	OBP	SLG
1,879	.293	.406	.537
Hits	HR	RBI	SB
1,905	366	1,234	86

PETER BOURJOS

Trust in the LORD with all your heart and lean not on your own understanding.

PROVERBS 3:5

This verse helps me calm down. There's so much going on in baseball and in life that you can't control, so when I read this verse, it puts me at peace. It puts everything in perspective for me.

I grew up Catholic. It's not that I didn't take it seriously, but I don't think a lot of kids enjoy going to church. When I got to St. Louis and met a lot of Christian players on the team, we would have Bible study once a week. That kind of got me going again and following Christ, and that changed my life. Things happen for a reason. When I got traded to the Cardinals, I didn't understand what that reason was; but when I left, I realized it was to bring me closer to Christ and get me back going to church and believing again. Adam Wainwright, Matt Holliday, and Mike Matheny are a good group of guys, and they do a good job of sticking together and building each other up.

Reading the Bible will change your life. You don't have to read it all. If you just read bits and pieces of it, you might pick something up and continue to grow. You're not going to learn everything in one day. That's something I realized. You are always evolving. If you can just read a little bit here and there, you will continue to grow in the Word.

Peter Bourjos

POSITION Outfielder

HEIGHT 6 foot 1

WEIGHT 185 lbs

BATS Right

THROWS Right

NUMBER 17

BORN March 31, 1987, in Park Ridge, Illinois

HIGH SCHOOL Notre Dame Prep (Scottsdale, Arizona)

COLLEGE American River College

DRAFTED Los Angeles Angels in 10th round of the 2005 amateur draft

HONORS 2010 Pacific Coast League Rookie of the Year

TEAMS Los Angeles Angels (2010–13); St. Louis Cardinals (2014–15); Philadelphia Phillies (2016–)

Bourjos' father, Chris, is a scout for the San Diego Padres.

Peter Bourjos is an excellent defensive outfielder and speedster who had his best season in 2011 with the Angels. He batted .271 and tied for the American League lead with 11 triples.

CAREER STATS

BATTING			
Games	AVG	OBP	SLG
713	.243	.300	.382
Hits	HR	RBI	SB
447	37	149	61

MATT BOYD

"Call to me and I will answer you and tell you great and unsearchable things you do not know."

JEREMIAH 33:3

I was fortunate enough to grow up in a Christian home. I had parents and grandparents who had faith, so I was really blessed that I had examples all around me of people who were walking with Christ. But it wasn't until college that I started to truly want to live my life in every aspect for Christ. I was aware of my actions and how they were to glorify His kingdom and to worship His name.

We have a strong fellowship on this team. We have believers and people of different faiths. Because of the platform we have, there's a risk/reward. You have the opportunity to influence a lot of people in a positive way. At the same time, with the fame and money, you can start worshipping false idols, and that might be the toughest thing at this level when you're living this dream.

He's always with you everywhere, in everything you do. Christ doesn't stop at the church doors, nor does He avoid the locker room. He's everywhere with you. He loves you regardless, and whatever happens, He always loves you and you are redeemed in Him. There's nothing you can do to lose that. He paid the price. Because of that, you're new in Christ. There's no reason to be discouraged, and if you live your life to glorify Him, you really can't lose at anything. You're already a champion in the game of life.

Matt Boyd

POSITION	Pitcher
HEIGHT	6 foot 3
WEIGHT	215 lbs
BATS	Left
THROWS	Left
NUMBER	48
BORN	February 2, 1991, in Bellevue, Washington
HIGH SCHOOL	Eastside Catholic (Sammamish, Washington)
COLLEGE	Oregon State University
DRAFTED	By Toronto Blue Jays in 6th round of 2013 amateur draft
HONORS	2015 Double-A All-Star
TEAMS	Toronto Blue Jays (2015); Detroit Tigers (2015–)

Boyd is a distant relative of Hall of Famer Bob Feller and former First Lady of the United States, Dolly Madison.

Matt Boyd was part of the trade that sent David Price from Detroit to Toronto in 2014. The left-hander had his best season for the Tigers in 2016, winning six games and posting a 4.53 ERA.

CAREER STATS

PITCHING				
Games	GS	W	L	CG
33	30	7	11	0
SHO	SV	ERA	IP	K
0	0	5.64	154.2	125

BLAINE BOYER

I sought the LORD, and he answered me;
he delivered me from all my fears.

PSALM 34:4

Once we come to the decision to accept Jesus as our Savior, tons of people believe all of a sudden our lives will be easier. But it's quite the opposite. We experience everyday life battles but also spiritual warfare battles. It helps when you recognize that you are unbelievably flawed as an individual living throughout the flesh and you need God. As athletes, we go through physical battles with people in competition, so I've always leaned on this verse. I read Psalms a lot when I was young in my faith, and it seemed I could really grasp what David was trying to say and the things he struggled with—the things he dealt with. This verse is such a grind verse. When you talk about fears, that's everything we deal with today. Whether it's competition, the middle of a bad situation, or any sort of warfare, we are called to lean on Him.

If people were around me when I'm alone, they would think I'm a lunatic because I'm holding conversations with Jesus out loud. You can see me when I'm on the mound. I'm always talking, constantly pleading for help. It's great to have a relationship with Him. It's not about a religion. Jesus came to abolish religion, to defeat the whole religious ideal. If my two sons told me they loved me every night at the same exact time right before they went to sleep and they did that for the rest of their lives, it would be meaningless at some point. Same thing if I did that to them. It would become an act with nothing behind it. God wants a relationship, constant dialogue. Even if you're ticked off, yell at Him. That's what He wants. He wants that intimate relationship with the people He loves. That's when the walk becomes real.

Blaine Boyer

POSITION	Pitcher
HEIGHT	6 foot 3
WEIGHT	225 lbs
BATS	Right
THROWS	Right
NUMBER	48
BORN	July 11, 1981, in Atlanta, Georgia
HIGH SCHOOL	Walton (Marietta, Georgia)
DRAFTED	By Atlanta Braves in 3rd round of 2000 amateur draft
HONORS	Honorable mention All-American centerfielder, as well as All-County and All-State in high school
TEAMS	Atlanta Braves (2005–09); St. Louis Cardinals (2009); Arizona Diamondbacks (2009–10); New York Mets (2011); San Diego Padres (2014); Minnesota Twins (2015); Milwaukee Brewers (2016–)

SEVENTH INNING STRETCH

Boyer spent 10 days in southeast Asia in November 2015 working undercover with former major league first baseman, Adam LaRoche, helping to identify and rescue underage sex slaves.

Blaine Boyer is a well-traveled pitcher who has pitched for seven major league teams and also played in Japan. His best season was 2015 with the Twins when he posted a 2.49 ERA in 68 appearances.

CAREER STATS

PITCHING				
Games	GS	W	L	CG
394	0	14	25	0
SHO	SV	ERA	IP	K
0	0	4.17	405.1	250

PAUL BYRD

"So if the Son sets you free, you will be free indeed."

JOHN 8:36

Jesus came not just to save us, but for freedom so we may have abundant life. We're not setting ourselves free; He's setting us free. So if I'm struggling with certain sins and things I can't kick, and I'm not home yet, I'm on the road, and I'm battling and trying to walk with God, it gives me great confidence to know that He's the one who is responsible for setting me free. And He has. And it's my job to believe and live it. If it's up to me to set me free, then we're all in trouble.

I was a guy who said a prayer to receive Christ about thirty-five times, but I kept struggling with different things. Eventually I realized I'm not perfect. I need to relax.

Usually the Christians are the ones who are more beat up and realize they need a Savior, so you can't expect them to do a one-eighty and be like Jesus the next day.

When I started experiencing God and interacting with Him, He changed me, and I wanted to be like Him. I found out God is so awesome, and having a relationship with Him made me want to change my life.

Paul Byrd

POSITION	Pitcher
HEIGHT	6 foot 1
WEIGHT	185 lbs
BATS	Right
THROWS	Right
NUMBER	36
BORN	December 3, 1970, in Louisville, Kentucky
HIGH SCHOOL	St. Xavier (Louisville, Kentucky)
COLLEGE	Louisiana State University
DRAFTED	By Cleveland Indians in the 4th round of the 1991 amateur draft
HONORS	1999 National League All-Star
TEAMS	New York Mets (1995–96); Atlanta Braves (1997–98, 2004); Philadelphia Phillies (1998–2001); Kansas City Royals (2001–02); Los Angeles Angels (2005); Cleveland Indians (2006–08); Boston Red Sox (2008–09)

Byrd has written a book called *Free Byrd* about his life, career, faith, and struggles.

After winning 12 games combined in his first four seasons, Paul Byrd had a breakout year with the Phillies in 1999. He won 15 games and was selected for the All-Star game that season. Byrd had five more seasons of double-digit wins and pitched for four teams in the postseason.

CAREER STATS

PITCHING				
Games	GS	W	L	CG
345	256	109	96	17
SHO	SV	ERA	IP	K
6	0	4.41	1,697	923

ADAM CONLEY

After this, the word of the LORD came to Abram in a vision: "Do not be afraid, Abram. I am your shield, your very great reward."

GENESIS 15:1

This whole chapter in Genesis is the most thorough example of the Gospels in the Old Testament. It's the most powerful scripture in my walk. When I think about the context of the entire chapter and how bizarre that may have been, it's unbelievably powerful. When you read it the first time, it's hard to know what it means.

I believe that every word of the Bible is true; so if I believe that God raised Jesus from the dead and Jesus is who He says He is, then everything in my life is prearranged, everything from my motivation behind things to who I am as a person to how I interact with people. Everything is shaded in a different light because I believe that's true. So my life isn't about me gaining for my status, for my joy, for my comfort, for my fame, for any of those things. I have to start looking at my purpose as a created being. If I can spend an eternity in paradise with a God who loves me, then it has to drastically affect the way I live my life because my life will be over in an eye blink.

So when I read this story in Genesis 15, it is the same God who was in the first century, and He is a God who is faithful, a God who is steadfast. He's always been the same, and Genesis 15 is just an illustration of His plan. That helps me not worry about stuff because He's been doing the same work He was doing thousands of years ago. So I feel pretty good that He knows what He's doing and He's got things under control. To see God's character on display here changes everything.

Adam Conley

POSITION	Pitcher
HEIGHT	6 foot 3
WEIGHT	200 lbs
BATS	Left
THROWS	Left
NUMBER	61
BORN	May 24, 1990, in Redmond, Washington
HIGH SCHOOL	Olympia (Olympia, Washington)
COLLEGE	Washington State University
DRAFTED	By Florida Marlins in 2nd round of 2011 amateur draft
HONORS	Miami's Organizational Pitcher of the Year 2015
TEAMS	Miami Marlins (2015–)

Conley started a regular season game when the Marlins played at Fort Bragg on July 3, 2016. It was the first time an MLB game was played at an active military base. He pitched six innings, allowed no runs, and was the winning pitcher.

Adam Conley was named to the midseason and postseason Pacific Coast All-Star teams in 2015 and made his major league debut that season. He beat the Reds on July 11, 2015, for his first career win in his second appearance.

CAREER STATS

PITCHING				
Games	GS	W	L	CG
40	36	12	7	0
SHO	SV	ERA	IP	K
0	0	3.82	200.1	183

CHRIS DAVIS

Therefore, since we are surrounded by such a great cloud of witnesses, let us throw off everything that hinders and the sin that so easily entangles. And let us run with perseverance the race marked out for us, fixing our eyes on Jesus, the pioneer and perfecter of faith. For the joy set before him he endured the cross, scorning its shame, and sat down at the right hand of the throne of God.

HEBREWS 12:1–2

I have this verse tattooed on my right rib cage. It's a constant reminder that we will face many difficult things in life that are hard for us to understand, but anything that we encounter, Christ has already experienced and overcome. We must remember to put our faith in the Lord and continue to persevere.

For many years, my mentality was there's nothing I can't overpower, overcome, with my own strength. God wants you to work hard and give all you have, but He also wants you to let go and surrender to Him. I really had to learn to do that and let Him control the results. Early in my career, I was hanging on to baseball so much. It was everything to me. If I was failing at baseball, I was failing at life. That's kind of where I was able to let go and let God take control.

Chris Davis

POSITION	First baseman
HEIGHT	6 foot 3
WEIGHT	230 lbs
BATS	Left
THROWS	Right
NUMBER	19
BORN	March 17, 1986, in Longview, Texas
HIGH SCHOOL	Longview (Longview, Texas)
COLLEGE	Navarro College
DRAFTED	By Texas Rangers in 5th round of the 2006 amateur draft
HONORS	2013 American League All-Star, Silver Slugger Award winner
TEAMS	Texas Rangers (2008–11); Baltimore Orioles (2011–)

Davis's nickname is "Crush."

Chris Davis became a prolific slugger once he was traded to Baltimore after playing a few seasons in the major leagues. Davis set a team record with 53 home runs in 2013.

CAREER STATS

BATTING			
Games	AVG	OBP	SLG
1,040	.250	.330	.499
Hits	HR	RBI	SB
922	241	633	16

BRIAN DOZIER

*So whether you eat or drink or whatever
you do, do it all for the glory of God.*

1 CORINTHIANS 10:31

From February to October, we are playing baseball every single day, and you have so many ups and downs. My turning point came in 2010 when I came across this verse.

Once I really embraced that, I didn't worry about hits anymore. I don't worry about homers. I don't worry about anything. If I go zero for five with five strikeouts but I still carry myself in a Christlike manner and influence somebody else, that's a beautiful day.

At home in Minnesota, the team has Tuesday Bible studies, and we really dig deep for an hour or so. We get together often, and sometimes we try to get together at somebody's house once a month. It's always good to do that, and sometimes we don't even open our Bibles. We just talk about real-life situations and how God is working in our lives.

I grew up in a Christian home. My grandparents, mom and dad, brother and sister, everybody was a Christian. I'm very blessed to have grown up with people around me who took me to church, but once I turned eleven, I realized that just because I'm a good person and try to live my life right, it doesn't mean I'm saved. One day we were at a Bible study with my mom, and when we got in the car, I told her I wanted to give my life to Christ. We turned back around and went to church, and I was baptized right there.

Brian Dozier

POSITION	Second baseman
HEIGHT	5 foot 11
WEIGHT	200 lbs
BATS	Right
THROWS	Right
NUMBER	2
BORN	May 15, 1987, in Tupelo, Mississippi
HIGH SCHOOL	Itawamba Agricultural (Fulton, Mississippi)
COLLEGE	University of Southern Mississippi
DRAFTED	By Minnesota Twins in 8th round of the 2009 amateur draft
HONORS	2015 American League All-Star
TEAMS	Minnesota Twins (2012–)

Dozier became the 16th player in major league history to hit a home run in his first career at-bat in the 2015 All-Star game.

Brian Dozier has emerged as one of the top sluggers in the majors. He set an American League record for second baseman by hitting 42 home runs in 2016.

CAREER STATS

BATTING			
Games	AVG	OBP	SLG
699	.246	.320	.442
Hits	HR	RBI	SB
668	117	346	74

MIKE DUNN

Jesus answered, "I am the way and the truth and the life.
No one comes to the Father except through me."

JOHN 14:6

In one little sentence, Jesus tells you there's no other way to heaven except through Him. No one can boast. No one is better than anyone else. Everyone is made the same in God's eyes. Everyone is equal, no matter your race, gender, or anything. It's about doing what you can for the Lord while you're here on earth. Jesus will get you to heaven. The road to hell is wide. It's an interstate, fifteen lanes wide. The road to heaven is one way. Being a Christian isn't going to make your life easy. It doesn't say: "Follow me and everything will be sunshine and roses." No, it's probably going to be harder because you separate yourself from the world and are unique to Jesus. He's your one-way street to heaven. There's no back road.

You can look at all these bad things that happen in the world and try to figure out why they are happening, but God has complete control over everything. He allows things to happen for the greater good, so no matter what's going on, try to find the good in it. Obviously, there's pain; there's suffering. If there's a death, hopefully that person knew Jesus and is in heaven with other family members. Dig deeper in the Word. Don't look at just the surface. Don't listen to what the world is telling you. Investigate for yourself. It's right there in the Bible. You can't earn your way to heaven. The only way is to go through Jesus. He took the punishment for us. We're all sinners. It's our nature. Repent, ask for forgiveness, and you will be saved.

Mike Dunn

POSITION	Pitcher
HEIGHT	6 foot
WEIGHT	183 lbs
BATS	Right
THROWS	Left
NUMBER	40
BORN	May 23, 1985, in Farmington, New Mexico
HIGH SCHOOL	Cimarron-Memorial (Las Vegas, Nevada)
COLLEGE	Southern Nevada
DRAFTED	By New York Yankees in 33rd round of 2004 amateur draft
HONORS	Tied for first in majors with ten relief wins in 2014
TEAMS	New York Yankees (2009), Atlanta Braves (2010), Miami Marlins (2011–)

Dunn originally signed as a position player and was converted to pitcher in 2006.

Mike Dunn is one of the toughest left-handed relievers in the majors. He had a career-best 2.66 ERA in 2013 and won ten games out of the bullpen the following season.

CAREER STATS

PITCHING				
Games	GS	W	L	CG
434	0	28	25	0
SHO	SV	ERA	IP	K
0	4	3.54	351	389

ZACH EFLIN

I didn't have the easiest life growing up with my family, and this verse has guided me through everything. Always walk by faith and always do everything you can through faith and you're going to get rewarded. I believe the Bible is such a great tool for me, as a human being, to be able to appreciate the Word and spread it throughout baseball and to everyone I encounter. I'm a big believer in that. I pray all the time, and this verse speaks to me.

I try to be a good person and spread the Word of God, so I don't think it should be considered a bold thing to do that. All people need God in their lives. It's sad to watch the world trend away from God, but the people who understand it are the people who believe and appreciate the Word of God.

Christ has given me such a peace of mind and an open heart and has really brought me down to earth and allowed me to appreciate everything in my life. I love reading the Bible and praying. It's changed me as a person in that I treat people better and look at things differently. I just think it's something you have to have and need to have, so I encourage everyone to do it.

Zach Eflin

POSITION	Pitcher
HEIGHT	6 foot 6
WEIGHT	215 lbs
BATS	Right
THROWS	Right
NUMBER	56
BORN	April 8, 1994, in Orlando, Florida
HIGH SCHOOL	Paul J. Hagerty (Oviedo, Florida)
DRAFTED	By San Diego Padres in 1st round (33rd overall) of 2012 amateur draft
HONORS	Triple-A Pitcher of the Week (April 11–18, 2016)
TEAMS	Philadelphia Phillies (2016–)

Eflin's paternal grandfather is a pastor.

Zach Eflin was part of two trades for star players, Matt Kemp and Jimmy Rollins, in a two-day span in December 2014. He reached the major leagues in 2016 and rebounded from an awful debut to pitch well for the Phillies, including two complete games and a shutout in July. Eflin's season ended early because he had surgery on both knees.

CAREER STATS

PITCHING				
Games	GS	W	L	CG
11	11	3	5	2
SHO	SV	ERA	IP	K
1	0	5.54	63.1	31

MAIKEL FRANCO

Jesus answered, "I am the way and the truth and the life. No one comes to the Father except through me."

JOHN 14:6

I like this verse because God is everything for me. When you have a good relationship with God, it's amazing because everything is going to be fine. Even if you have a tough moment in your life, you have to thank God for everything. You have to thank Him for your food, for a new day, for your life, for your family. The only thing you can control is how you live your life every day. God is the path to truth and life. If you believe Jesus died for your sins and you give your life to Him, He is the way to heaven.

I always pray when I wake up in the morning, when I go to sleep, during games. I don't really pray for myself. I pray for everybody to stay away from injury, and I pray for my family. Sometimes I need something and I take the time to pray about it, but I may not get what I want because Jesus has the right time and the perfect moment, and you have to understand that.

I know I have a lot of fans and young kids following me, and it's been amazing. I want them to know in tough moments, you can't do it alone. Pray to Jesus, and give Him control. He is the way.

Maikel Franco

POSITION	Third baseman
HEIGHT	6 foot 1
WEIGHT	215 lbs
BATS	Right
THROWS	Right
NUMBER	7
BORN	August 26, 1992, in Azua, Dominican Republic
SIGNED	By Philadelphia Phillies as amateur free agent in 2010
HONORS	National League Rookie of the Month (June 2015)
TEAMS	Philadelphia Phillies (2014–)

SEVENTH INNING STRETCH

Franco's first hit was a single off Stephen Strasburg on September 12, 2014.

Maikel Franco is a hard-hitting third baseman who is considered a cornerstone player of the future for the Phillies. Franco had an outstanding rookie season shortened by injury in 2015 and followed up with a solid year, hitting 25 homers and driving in 88 runs.

CAREER STATS

BATTING			
Games	AVG	OBP	SLG
248	.259	.312	.437
Hits	HR	RBI	SB
243	39	143	2

JEFF FRANCOEUR

"Have I not commanded you? Be strong and courageous.
Do not be afraid; do not be discouraged,
for the LORD your God will be with you wherever you go."

JOSHUA 1:9

On July 7, 2004, I was in the minor leagues and I got hit in the face with a ninety-six-mile-per-hour fastball. I had a six-hour surgery. And I was mad. I was a Christian at the time, but I was mad at God. I was thinking I had it all planned out; I was getting ready to get to the big leagues and that happened. But my mom read me this verse in the hospital every day. And one of the days she read it, it finally clicked, and it's been my life verse ever since. Sometimes I write it on my batting gloves when I give them to kids to let them know what's most important in my life.

If you talk to most Christians in this game, you'll see a happiness that's a lot different from other people. Yeah, we're competitive, we get frustrated, we get mad; but at the end of the day, you know you have a greater cause than one that amounts to nine innings and playing ball. There's a lot more to life, and it's bringing people to the kingdom. Getting in the Word is the best way to do it. Whenever you feel bad, there's nothing that makes you feel better than reading the Bible. You know you have someone who died for you.

As a Christian, you should feel even more freed up because if you're reading the Word, doing the things you should, and getting closer to God, you understand His grace and mercy, and that's the only way to the altar.

Jeff Francoeur

POSITION	Outfielder
HEIGHT	6 foot 4
WEIGHT	225 lbs
BATS	Right
THROWS	Right
NUMBER	5
BORN	January 8, 1984, in Atlanta, Georgia
HIGH SCHOOL	Parkview (Lilburn, Georgia)
DRAFTED	By Atlanta Braves in 1st round (23rd overall) of the 2002 amateur draft
HONORS	Finished third in National League Rookie of the Year voting in 2005; 2007 National League Gold Glove Award winner
TEAMS	Atlanta Braves (2005–09); New York Mets (2009–10); Texas Rangers (2010); Kansas City Royals (2011–13); San Francisco Giants (2013); San Diego Padres (2014); Philadelphia Phillies (2015), Braves (2016); Miami Marlins (2016–)

Jeff Francoeur broke into the majors with the Braves as a heralded prospect and had a couple outstanding seasons before bouncing around the majors. Known for a strong arm, a solid glove, and being an excellent presence in the clubhouse, Francoeur is a popular teammate and a player managers want on their team.

CAREER STATS

BATTING			
Games	AVG	OBP	SLG
1,479	.261	.304	.416
Hits	HR	RBI	SB
1,373	160	698	54

SCOOTER GENNETT

Whoever claims to love God yet hates a brother or sister is a liar. For whoever does not love their brother and sister, whom they have seen, cannot love God, whom they have not seen.

1 JOHN 4:20

This verse puts it all together. You have to love everyone, whether they are a friend, acquaintance, an enemy, or a family member. Even when someone makes it hard for you to love him or her, you have to try to be there for that person. That's all Jesus was trying to do. Whether it was a sick person, a homeless guy, a tax collector, or whoever, He was trying to be there for everyone and get them to understand that life is about helping others and being the best person you can be. I believe our job is to show people the Word, to try to bring them closer to God, and to be good examples as Christians. The worst thing I could do as a Christian is to go out and not play the game the right way and not sign autographs for people. Those are things in my control, and they may not necessarily reflect that I'm a Christian, but once they find out and they see the respect I have for the game on the field, they'll know.

Throughout most of my career, I would chew smokeless tobacco until I realized all these kids are watching me play. It was so selfish of me to chew, and I didn't want to set the wrong example anymore, so I just stopped. It was more about being a good example than my heath and concerns about mouth cancer. Now if I get that urge to chew, I pop in bubblegum or sunflower seeds. If the urge gets so strong to the point where I want to stop at a gas station and buy some, I go to God and pray. We're around tobacco all the time. Being on TV, being in the public eye, I didn't want people to see me do that, knowing that I'm a Christian, and let that steer them away from Jesus.

Scooter Gennett

POSITION	Second baseman
HEIGHT	5 foot 10
WEIGHT	185 lbs
BATS	Left
THROWS	Right
NUMBER	2
BORN	May 1, 1990, in Cincinnati, Ohio
HIGH SCHOOL	Sarasota (Sarasota, Florida)
DRAFTED	By Milwaukee Brewers in 16th round of the 2009 amateur draft
HONORS	2011 Single-A All-Star, 2012 Double-A All-Star
TEAMS	Milwaukee Brewers (2013–)

Gennett's first name is Ryan.
He got the nickname Scooter as a
kid watching "Muppet Babies."

Scooter Gennett began his career as a platoon infielder before becoming an everyday player in 2016 when he had career highs in homers (14) and runs batted in (56).

CAREER STATS

BATTING			
Games	AVG	OBP	SLG
456	.279	.318	.420
Hits	HR	RBI	SB
426	35	160	17

KYLE GIBSON

*For it is by grace you have been saved, through faith—
and this is not from yourselves, it is the gift of God—not
by works, so that no one can boast. For we are God's
handiwork, created in Christ Jesus to do good works,
which God prepared in advance for us to do.*

EPHESIANS 2:8–10

When I give an autograph, I sign that verse because the whole message itself encompasses what I'm trying to do and why I'm on this earth to do what God put me here to do.

I had always gone to church my whole life, but when I was fifteen, I had an arm injury, and it was the first time I couldn't lean on baseball. To that point, baseball had been my identity. I ended up going to a church camp that summer, and I decided to give my life to Christ and started following Him. It's been a journey ever since. It turned out what I thought was going to be one of the worst summers ended up one of the best. It gave me a little different focus on life and allowed me to understand some things are more important than others. It gave me a good foundation for day-to-day life and how to deal with failure and success and being a light and spreading the love of Jesus to the people around me.

It's important to just follow Him, read about Him, and talk to Him. All sixty-six books of the Bible are important, but Matthew, Mark, Luke, and John are probably the most important ones because they walk you through four perspectives on the life of Christ, the guy we're all supposed to be trying to follow. If you have never experienced that, start there, and it's amazing what you'll find when you start paying attention to how He lived and the advice He gives us because everything we need to know is in those four books.

Kyle Gibson

POSITION	Pitcher
HEIGHT	6 foot 6
WEIGHT	215 lbs
BATS	Right
THROWS	Right
NUMBER	44
BORN	October 23, 1987, in Greenfield, Indiana
HIGH SCHOOL	Greenfield Central (Greenfield, Indiana)
DRAFTED	By Minnesota Twins in 1st round (22nd overall) of 2009 amateur draft
HONORS	2010 Twins Minor League Pitcher of the Year
TEAMS	Minnesota Twins (2013–)

Kyle Gibson won 13 games in his first full season in the majors with the Twins in 2014 and followed up with an 11-win season the next year. The lanky right-hander slumped in 2016 but finished strong with a 3.70 ERA in his last four starts.

CAREER STATS

PITCHING				
Games	GS	W	L	CG
98	98	32	38	2
SHO	SV	ERA	IP	K
0	0	4.59	572.1	385

JEANMAR GOMEZ

And we know that in all things God works for the good of those who love him, who have been called according to his purpose.

ROMANS 8:28

I grew up in a Christian house because my grandma was a Christian for sixty years. She was the founder of a church in Venezuela. God used my grandma to speak to me about faith, and God has been with me always no matter where I go. I'm so thankful to be a Christian.

The Bible says we should be thankful for everything. I know that every opportunity I have is from God. The opportunity to play in the major leagues, the opportunity to pitch for the Phillies, it's all from Him. I'm very thankful. I try to do my best to prepare before games, and once I enter the game, I just trust in God. Whatever He has planned for me for that moment, I'm thankful no matter the situation because He works for my good like this verse says. You have to have faith in Him for everything.

And when you have the opportunity to speak the Word of God with another player, you have to speak with confidence and tell them what Jesus has done in your life and what He did for all of us. Sometimes when a teammate has a tough moment, you have to tell them about God and help them get through the situation.

I like to encourage children to just talk to God like a friend when they pray, read the Bible as much as they can, and have faith. My wife is pregnant, and that's such a blessing.

Jeanmar Gomez

POSITION	Pitcher
HEIGHT	6 foot 3
WEIGHT	215 lbs
BATS	Right
THROWS	Right
NUMBER	46
BORN	February 10, 1988, in Caracas, Distrito Federal, Venezuela
SIGNED	By Cleveland Indians as amateur free agent in 2005
HONORS	Ranked 5th in the National League in saves in 2016
TEAMS	Cleveland Indians (2010–12); Pittsburgh Pirates (2013–14); Philadelphia Phillies (2015–)

Gomez's entrance song during the 2016 season was "El Gran Yo Soy" by Julissa, the Spanish version of "Great I Am."

Jeanmar Gomez began his career as a starting pitcher before moving to the bullpen in 2013 with the Pirates. He became a closer for the Phillies in 2016 and had a breakout season in 2016, saving 37 games.

CAREER STATS

PITCHING				
Games	GS	W	L	CG
255	46	24	26	0
SHO	SV	ERA	IP	K
0	38	4.26	492.2	300

CHASE HEADLEY

For the Spirit God gave us does not make us timid,
but gives us power, love and self-discipline.

2 TIMOTHY 1:7

This verse encompasses what I want to do in my Christian walk. Christians are often portrayed as weak, and there's this misconception that we are supposed to be passive and maybe not compete as hard as other people. But this verse says the opposite. We are called to be warriors for Christ. In Christ, I have power to stand up as a Christian, to love even when it's hard to love the unlovable, and to have the self-discipline to resist the temptations we face daily. Professional athletes have a tremendous platform. There are a lot of challenges and different things pushing you in different directions when you have notoriety, so you have to be careful; but you want to use that platform and look for opportunities to speak out about being a Christian.

I came to Christ as a freshman in high school when I went to a meeting for the Fellowship of Christian Athletes. They talked about salvation. It was the first time I was really exposed to the Gospel, and I was saved. It's a huge part of my life.

My goal is to have Christ be the center of everything. I can worship Jesus by the way I play baseball and in how I interact with teammates, opponents, umpires, and fans.

Chase Headley

POSITION Third baseman

HEIGHT 6 foot 2

WEIGHT 215 lbs

BATS Both

THROWS Right

NUMBER 12

BORN May 9, 1984, in Fountain, Colorado

HIGH SCHOOL Fountain-Fort Carson (Fountain, Colorado)

COLLEGE University of Tennessee, University of the Pacific

DRAFTED By San Diego Padres in 2nd round of the 2005 amateur draft

HONORS 2012 National League Gold Glove Award winner, 2012 National League Silver Slugger Award winner

TEAMS San Diego Padres (2007–14); New York Yankees (2014–)

Headley was named the 2002 Male Athlete of the Year by the Fellowship of Christian Athletes.

A two-sport star in high school and class valedictorian, Chase Headley has been a solid third baseman in the major leagues for several years. He had a breakout season for the Padres in 2012 when he was fifth in voting for the MVP award.

CAREER STATS

BATTING			
Games	AVG	OBP	SLG
1,262	.263	.342	.401
Hits	HR	RBI	SB
1,190	118	531	84

CESAR HERNANDEZ

*"Have I not commanded you? Be strong and courageous.
Do not be afraid; do not be discouraged,
for the LORD your God will be with you wherever you go."*

JOSHUA 1:9

I like this verse because when you go through rough times, this verse tells you to be strong, be brave, don't fear anything, and keep your head up because God is with you wherever you are.

I have been a Christian since I was a little kid because my mom was a Christian, and she would always take us to church. When I grew up, I stopped going to church, but I always knew about God and I would fear Him. I thought this was good because when you fear God, you have Him in your heart.

When I came to the big leagues and met Jeanmar Gomez, I started to get closer and closer to God again, and I started going to church again. I'm thankful and blessed that I didn't have to go through a tough time before I came back to God.

God knows what the future holds, but you don't, so you have to keep chasing your dreams and don't fear doing what He wants you to do. You have to trust God, be faithful, and things will happen for you.

Cesar Hernandez

POSITION Second baseman

HEIGHT 5 foot 10

WEIGHT 160 lbs

BATS Both

THROWS Right

NUMBER 16

BORN May 23, 1990, in Valencia, Carabobo, Venezuela

SIGNED By Philadelphia Phillies as amateur free agent in 2006

HONORS 2012 Double-A All-Star

TEAMS Philadelphia Phillies (2013–)

SEVENTH INNING STRETCH

Hernandez signed with the Phillies on July 2, 2006, along with native Venezulean, Freddy Galvis, his current double-play partner.

Cesar Hernandez began his career as a versatile utility player but developed into a solid starting second baseman during the 2016 season when he led the Phillies with a .294 batting average, hit 11 triples, and posted a .371 on-base percentage.

CAREER STATS

BATTING			
Games	AVG	OBP	SLG
382	.281	.350	.361
Hits	HR	RBI	SB
333	8	88	37

MATT HOLLIDAY

"Where were you when I laid the earth's foundation? Tell me, if you understand."

JOB 38:4

Being a Christian is the cornerstone of who I am. It's my top priority. My relationship with Jesus is a handbook of how to live your life through the Bible. Being a husband, father, and teammate, you get a chance to witness and be a man of God and be the best man you can be and live your life for Him. How you treat people shows the impact God has had on your life. When you are submissive to the Lord, your life falls in better order. Obviously, I fall short every day, but striving to live a life that honors Him is my first priority.

When I gave my life to Christ and started trying to live for Him and stopped living for me, I started considering other people's feelings more than I had in the past. I realized I had been selfish, and I learned that God has a plan for all of us. I work hard and do all the things I can, but at the same time, His will is perfect, and me trying to control it is not going to work.

Matt Holliday

POSITION	Outfielder
HEIGHT	6 foot 4
WEIGHT	240 lbs
BATS	Right
THROWS	Right
NUMBER	7
BORN	January 15, 1980, in Stillwater, Oklahoma
HIGH SCHOOL	Stillwater (Stillwater, Oklahoma)
DRAFTED	By Colorado Rockies in 7th round of 1998 amateur draft
HONORS	Seven-time All-Star, 2007 National League championship series Most Valuable Player, four-time Silver Slugger Award winner
TEAMS	Colorado Rockies (2004–08); Oakland A's (2009); St. Louis Cardinals (2009–16)

Holliday was labeled a "can't miss" prospect by former NFL coach Jimmy Johnson as a high school quarterback.

Matt Holliday is among the most consistent, best hitters in baseball. Holliday batted over .300 five straight seasons and won a batting title with a .340 average in 2007 when he led the Rockies to a National League pennant. Holliday joined the Cardinals in 2009 and helped them win a World Series title two years later.

CAREER STATS

BATTING			
Games	AVG	OBP	SLG
1,773	.303	.382	.515
Hits	HR	RBI	SB
1,995	295	1,153	107

ENDER INCIARTE

Where I come from, Venezuela, it's very hard for someone to make it here and reach the major leagues. We go through a lot of things to get here, and then we go through a lot in the minors to get to where we are, so this verse is a reminder that we are not alone. Growing up, it was a dream to make it to the major leagues, but once it happened, I couldn't believe it. I'm really grateful and thankful to be here, and I do everything I can to stay here.

My mom was always the biggest Christian, and she had a lot of faith. She encouraged me to follow God, so every second, every day, every year, I try to get closer to Him and get to know Him better.

Religion is just a word. My religion is God, so I try to play for Him. Hopefully one day, people can see Him through me. I try to become a better person, a better example; because if I follow Him, I have to set an example for others.

I encourage others to read the Bible, because if you can keep the faith and have a good mindset, you can do whatever you want to do in life.

Ender Inciarte

POSITION	Outfielder
HEIGHT	5 foot 11
WEIGHT	190 lbs
BATS	Left
THROWS	Left
NUMBER	11
BORN	October 29, 1990, in Maracaibo, Zulia, Venezuela
SIGNED	By Arizona Diamondbacks as amateur free agent in 2008
HONORS	Finished 5th in voting for 2014 National League Rookie of the Year
TEAMS	Philadelphia Phillies (2013); Arizona Diamondbacks (2014); Atlanta Braves (2015–)

SEVENTH INNING STRETCH

Inciarte was on the Phillies' roster for the 2013 season opener but didn't play and returned to Arizona after one game.

A Venezuelan native, Ender Inciarte has developed into one of the top leadoff hitters in his first three seasons in the majors. He ranked ninth in the National League with a .303 batting average in 2015 and followed up with a .291 average in 2016.

CAREER STATS

BATTING			
Games	AVG	OBP	SLG
381	.292	.337	.385
Hits	HR	RBI	SB
427	13	101	56

DON KELLY

*Do not conform to the pattern of this world,
but be transformed by the renewing of your mind.
Then you will be able to test and approve what
God's will is—his good, pleasing and perfect will.*

ROMANS 12:2

For us in baseball, and in life, to be able to focus on Christ, to focus on transforming our minds, to focus on the right things, it puts you in a good place to be successful.

Baseball is such a game of failure. You have slumps, and you have to try to be consistent. I always try to keep in mind that a bad game is a reminder to lean on Him through the good times and the bad. You have to focus on the things Christ called us to focus on and stay positive and try to live your life that way. That's how I try to approach it. It's harder to lean on Him when everything else is smooth. In life you go through tough times. God takes those things that may put us in what we think is a bad situation and ultimately use them for good. I am comforted knowing I am where God wants me.

I was saved when I was eight years old, but I rededicated myself to Christ through baseball after going through injuries. It's been awesome ever since. Jesus Christ is my rock.

Don Kelly

POSITION	First baseman, third baseman, outfielder
HEIGHT	6 foot 4
WEIGHT	215 lbs
BATS	Left
THROWS	Right
NUMBER	31
BORN	February 15, 1980, in Butler, Pennsylvania
HIGH SCHOOL	Mount Lebanon (Mount Lebanon, Pennsylvania)
COLLEGE	Point Park Nazarene University
DRAFTED	By Detroit Tigers in 8th round of the 2001 amateur draft
HONORS	Tigers 2013 Heart and Hustle Award winner
TEAMS	Pittsburgh Pirates (2007); Detroit Tigers (2009–14); Miami Marlins (2014–)

New York Mets second baseman
Neil Walker is Kelly's brother-in-law.

A versatile player known for being a positive
influence on teammates, Don Kelly is the only
active player to have played every position on
the field, including pitcher.

CAREER STATS

BATTING			
Games	AVG	OBP	SLG
585	.230	.294	.334
Hits	HR	RBI	SB
252	23	98	16

IAN KENNEDY

"For I know the plans I have for you," declares the LORD, "plans to prosper you and not to harm you, plans to give you hope and a future."

JEREMIAH 29:11

When I was struggling with the Yankees in 2008 and I was sent back down to the minor leagues, this verse came up in my wife's reading plan, and it popped out to us. We don't know God's whole plan. I felt I was getting closer and closer in my walk with Jesus, yet I was feeling so far away from Him. Baseball is something I was passionate about, and I felt it was being pulled away from me. I realized I was holding baseball so tight and I didn't want to let it go. I gave everything else up (to Christ), but I didn't give the game up to Him, and I wanted to control it myself. I didn't know how to combine my walk and baseball, and I learned that season it all goes together. It's all His. He gave me this talent. He allowed me to play this game. What I had to do was give it up to Him and not hold it so tight. That verse really stuck with me because I didn't understand why I was struggling, why I lived out of a suitcase for so long. It was something I had to go through for His purpose, and I realized this was for His glory.

I wish I would've known Jesus a lot earlier in my life. I grew up Catholic. I knew why we celebrated Easter. I knew the Catholic teachings. I went to church occasionally. I had a lot of questions in high school. I asked my mom one day, "How do we know the Bible is true?" We ended up going to a new church, and it answered a lot of questions. Before I turned seventeen, I told my mom I wanted to be baptized and I wanted to follow Jesus. I went to college and I was up and down, but still my idol was baseball. I met a chaplain who really challenged me, and I needed that. He helped me a lot, and he helped my wife, Allison.

Ian Kennedy

POSITION Pitcher

HEIGHT 6 foot

WEIGHT 200 lbs

BATS Right

THROWS Right

NUMBER 31

BORN December 19, 1984, in Huntington Beach, California

HIGH SCHOOL La Quinta (Westminster, California)

COLLEGE USC

DRAFTED By New York Yankees in 1st round (21st overall) of 2006 amateur draft

HONORS Finished 4th in voting for National League Cy Young Award in 2011 and was 14th in Most Valuable Player voting

TEAMS New York Yankees (2007–09); Arizona Diamondbacks (2010–13); San Diego Padres (2013–15); Kansas City Royals (2016–)

Kennedy walked 11 times as a hitter in 2012, the most walks by a pitcher in the last 30 years.

After being traded to Arizona as part of a three-team deal that sent Max Scherzer to Detroit, Ian Kennedy emerged as top starter with the Diamondbacks. He was 21–4 in 2011 and 15–12 in 2012, but was traded to San Diego during the 2013 season. He returned to the American League in 2016, joining Kansas City and remains an effective starting pitcher.

CAREER STATS

PITCHING				
Games	GS	W	L	CG
239	237	86	79	2
SHO	SV	ERA	IP	K
1	0	3.94	1,430.1	1,324

CLAYTON KERSHAW

I am so blessed to have the talent to play baseball, and I realize that. But God gives us our talent and abilities so we can glorify Him in everything we do. Since I was a kid, all I ever wanted to do was play in the major leagues. But why am I playing baseball? Everyone wants to have success and be a Hall of Famer. But then what? For me, it's about the legacy you leave off the field. It's about how many people I can affect with the platform God gave me.

Whether I'm pitching on a baseball mound or living my life outside of the baseball field, it's giving up my life to God that really puts my life in perspective. Being a Christian means you have to keep reminding yourself that you're supposed to stand out, you're supposed to be different, you're supposed to act boldly in your faith. It's not easy, but it's worth the fight.

Clayton Kershaw

POSITION	Pitcher
HEIGHT	6 foot 4
WEIGHT	225 lbs
BATS	Left
THROWS	Left
NUMBER	22
BORN	March 19, 1988, in Dallas, Texas
HIGH SCHOOL	Highland Park (University Park, Texas)
DRAFTED	By Los Angeles Dodgers in 1st round (7th overall) of the 2006 amateur draft
HONORS	Three-time National League Cy Young Award winner, 2014 National League Most Valuable Player, six-time All-Star, 2011 Gold Glove Award winner
TEAMS	Los Angeles Dodgers (2008–)

The average annual value of Kershaw's contract, $30.7 million, is the largest ever for a baseball player.

Clayton Kershaw is one of the most dominant pitchers in the majors. In 2014, the hard-throwing lefty became the first National League pitcher to be named MVP since Bob Gibson in 1968. Along with winning three Cy Young Awards, Kershaw has twice finished in the top 3 in voting.

CAREER STATS

PITCHING				
Games	GS	W	L	CG
265	263	126	60	24
SHO	SV	ERA	IP	K
15	0	2.37	1,760	1,918

PEDRO MARTINEZ

The LORD is my rock, my fortress and my deliverer; my God is my rock, in whom I take refuge, my shield and the horn of my salvation, my stronghold.

PSALM 18:2

As a kid growing up in the Dominican Republic, I used to pray all the time and ask God to help me become a baseball player. After the Dodgers signed me, some of the scouts questioned my ability because of my size. I was a very skinny kid. They said I was too small to develop. They said I wasn't strong enough to continue to throw hard. But God uses the weak to show the stronger ones who the power really belongs to, and I became one big example of what God wants to do.

He's God. He's the Mighty One. He's the only one who knows what we really are, and He has the power to help us overcome any limitations we think we have.

Pedro Martinez

POSITION Pitcher

HEIGHT 5 foot 11

WEIGHT 170 lbs

BATS Right

THROWS Right

NUMBER 45

BORN October 25, 1971, in Manoguayabo, Distrito Nacional, Dominican Republic

SIGNED By Los Angeles Dodgers as amateur free agent in 1988

HONORS Inducted into the Hall of Fame in 2015, eight-time All-Star, three-time Cy Young Award winner, 1999 All-Star Game Most Valuable Player

TEAMS Los Angeles Dodgers (1992–93); Montreal Expos (1994–97); Boston Red Sox (1998–2004); New York Mets (2005–08); Philadelphia Phillies (2009)

Martinez was the second Dominican
enshrined in the Hall of Fame,
joining Juan Marichal.

Pedro Martinez is one of the greatest pitchers of his generation. He won three Cy Young awards, including one in both leagues. He earned five pitching titles and the pitching triple crown in 1999 when he led the American League in wins, ERA, and strikeouts. Martinez helped the Red Sox capture the 2004 World Series and finished his career pitching in the 2009 World Series for the Phillies.

CAREER STATS

PITCHING				
Games	GS	W	L	CG
476	409	219	100	46
SHO	SV	ERA	IP	K
17	3	2.93	2,827.1	3,154

MIKE MATHENY

For I am not ashamed of the gospel, because it is the power of God that brings salvation to everyone who believes: first to the Jew, then to the Gentile.

ROMANS 1:16

I'm not ashamed of the Gospel of Christ, and I don't want to ever walk away from the opportunity to tell people about the great gift of grace that I've received.

We have an incredible mission field. It has bases and it's beautiful and fifty thousand people come root for us; but a baseball diamond is a mission field no different than any other, whether it's at school or the workplace. We, as Christians, have to take advantage of our mission field and share the Gospel, not by forcing it or pushing it on people, but through living life loving people and asking God to open doors that can make a difference, doors that lead to eternity.

I grew up in a strong Christian family and became very religious. But then I heard a pastor deliver a challenging sermon. He asked: "Do you know who Jesus is? Who is He to you?" That stuck with me. I was wrestling with God. I realized religion had become a routine, and I needed to develop a relationship with Christ. My parents led me through the Gospel, and I responded with faith on my own.

Mike Matheny

POSITION	Catcher
HEIGHT	6 foot 3
WEIGHT	205 lbs
BATS	Right
THROWS	Right
NUMBER	22
BORN	September 22, 1970, in Columbus, Ohio
HIGH SCHOOL	Reynoldsburg (Reynoldsburg, Ohio)
COLLEGE	University of Michigan
DRAFTED	By Milwaukee Brewers in 8th round of 1991 amateur draft
HONORS	Four-time Gold Glove Award winner
TEAMS	Milwaukee Brewers (1994–98); Toronto Blue Jays (1999); St. Louis Cardinals (2000–04); San Francisco Giants (2005–06)

Matheny is one of only three major league catchers to have an errorless season of at least 100 games.

Mike Matheny was a top defensive catcher throughout his major league career. Known for his leadership ability, Matheny was hired to replace the legendary Tony La Russa as manager of the Cardinals after the 2011 season. He became the first manager in baseball history to lead his team to the postseason in his first four seasons.

CAREER STATS

BATTING			
Games	AVG	OBP	SLG
1,305	.239	.293	.344
Hits	HR	RBI	SB
925	67	443	8

STEVEN MATZ

*And to make it your ambition to lead a quiet life:
You should mind your own business and work with
your hands, just as we told you, so that your daily life
may win the respect of outsiders and so that you
will not be dependent on anybody.*

1 THESSALONIANS 4:11–12

This verse talks about being self-sufficient in a secular kind of way. I want to be able to do things for myself in a worldly way so I can reach other people. Sometimes we're so involved in what other people are doing and we want what they have, but this verse reminds us to be humble and work hard, and that lines up with the way I want to live my life.

It's hard in this game because you never think it'll be so tough, and then you get to this level and there's a lot of demand for your time, demand for your attention, and sometimes you want to blow people off. But this verse tells me to mind my own business, work hard, and be humble.

When I realized it wasn't a matter of being a good person or bad person, that's when I became a better person because I realized I didn't have to work my way or earn my way (to heaven) but rather be a good person because Jesus loves me. Once I recognized that, it's been a slow change for me, and my mindset became completely different.

There is a way, and it's through Jesus and the Bible.

Steven Matz

POSITION	Pitcher
HEIGHT	6 foot 2
WEIGHT	200 lbs
BATS	Right
THROWS	Left
NUMBER	32
BORN	May 29, 1991, in Stony Brook, New York
HIGH SCHOOL	Ward Melville (East Setauket, New York)
DRAFTED	By New York Mets in 2nd round of 2009 amateur draft
HONORS	Mets Organizational Pitcher of the Year in 2014
TEAMS	New York Mets (2015–)

Matz is the only pitcher and the 26th player in the last century to collect at least four RBIs in his major league debut.

Steven Matz had perhaps the best major league debut by any pitcher in baseball history. He earned the win against the Reds on June 28, 2015, and was 3 for 3 with four RBIs. Matz pitched in only six games as a rookie and started Game 4 of the World Series. Matz was limited to only 22 starts in 2016 because of injuries.

CAREER STATS

PITCHING				
Games	GS	W	L	CG
28	28	13	8	0
SHO	SV	ERA	IP	K
0	0	3.16	168	163

ANDREW MCCUTCHEN

And we know that in all things God works for the good of those who love him, who have been called according to his purpose.

ROMANS 8:28

My dad is a pastor, and growing up he instilled this verse in me. It's what keeps me positive and keeps me going. It's amazing to look at where I came from to where I am now. I know God gave me talents to use to the best of my ability for His glory and to be able to help others. The game is not mine. It doesn't control me. I give it all to God. People say that when something happens to you with the Lord, you start to see things different. That's kind of the way I started seeing things; and the more I started to see things differently, the more my game took off and I had success.

I feel blessed beyond measure. I am thankful for every single day the Lord has given me and for what He did for me when He died on the cross for my sins.

If there is anything in life that you do or anything that you want, make God the center of your attention, and He will open your eyes to make things a lot easier for you to see. It makes failure easier to be able to encounter because you know God is there. You understand it's just an obstacle He put you through to get you where He wants you to go.

Andrew McCutchen

POSITION	Center fielder
HEIGHT	5 foot 10
WEIGHT	190 lbs
BATS	Right
THROWS	Right
NUMBER	22
BORN	October 10, 1986, in Fort Meade, Florida
HIGH SCHOOL	Fort Meade (Fort Meade, Florida)
DRAFTED	By Pittsburgh Pirates in 1st round (11th overall) of the 2005 amateur draft
HONORS	Five-time National League All-Star, 2013 National League Most Valuable Player, 2012 National League Gold Glove Award winner
TEAMS	Pittsburgh Pirates (2009–)

McCutchen cut his dreadlocks before the 2015 season, and proceeds from the sale of his hair benefited Pirates Charities.

Andrew McCutchen has been one of the best outfielders in the major leagues for nearly a decade, helping the Pirates end a long postseason drought and leading them to the playoffs three straight seasons between 2013–15.

CAREER STATS

BATTING			
Games	AVG	OBP	SLG
1,190	.292	.381	.487
Hits	HR	RBI	SB
1,304	175	637	160

DANIEL MURPHY

That's the Gospel. Jesus has done all the work. He died the death I deserved. The work is finished. We have peace and joy through Him and through His sacrifice. Now we get to enjoy Him because of His sacrifice that He made for us, the perfect blood He shed for our sins. So now I have peace, and I get to enjoy Him in my surrender to His will in my life. Jesus is a person. He lives.

My relationship is as strong or as weak as I want it to be because Jesus never moves. I'm always the one who decides how strong it is. Jesus is constant. He's steadfast. It's the same way when I want to get to know my wife—I speak to my wife, I communicate with my wife, and I try to understand her characteristics. When I want to know and understand Jesus more, I go to His living Word, the Bible, and I learn about Him and learn His characteristics. It's not a list of dos and dont's, because I can't keep them. He paid the price. It's cool that in that moment in each one of our lives when we feel helpless, when we feel we've lost control of a situation and can't do anything about it, Jesus says, "Perfect. I already paid for that. I control that."

Daniel Murphy

POSITION Second baseman

HEIGHT 6 foot 1

WEIGHT 220 lbs

BATS Left

THROWS Right

NUMBER 20

BORN April 1, 1985, in Jacksonville, Florida

HIGH SCHOOL Englewood Senior (Jacksonville, Florida)

COLLEGE Jacksonville University

DRAFTED By New York Mets in 13th round of the 2006 amateur draft

HONORS Two-time All-Star, 2015 National League championship series Most Valuable Player

TEAMS New York Mets (2008–15); Washington Nationals (2016–)

Jacksonville University was the only four-year school to offer Murphy a scholarship.

Daniel Murphy was already known for his excellent hitting before a breakout postseason in 2015 when he helped the Mets reach the World Series. Murphy set a major league record by hitting a home run in six consecutive postseason games. Murphy continued his hot hitting into his first season with Washington after signing as a free agent. He set career highs with a .347 batting average, 25 home runs, and 104 runs batted in to help the Nationals win a division title.

CAREER STATS

BATTING			
Games	AVG	OBP	SLG
1,045	.296	.339	.447
Hits	HR	RBI	SB
1,151	87	506	62

JIMMY NELSON

Consider it pure joy, my brothers and sisters, whenever you face trials of many kinds, because you know that the testing of your faith produces perseverance. Let perseverance finish its work so that you may be mature and complete, not lacking anything.

JAMES 1:2–4

This verse applies to everybody in the world because we all go through trials and tribulations. We've all gone through something—whether it's a tragedy or smaller trial—that has shaped us and strengthened our faith. The thing that hits me hard with this verse is the part that says: "Consider it pure joy" when you face troubled times, because how often are we actually happy that we're going through tough moments? Never. It especially applies in this game because baseball is built on failure and adjustments, so this verse really hits home for me. Also, I've had to overcome things in my past that have strengthened my faith and made me a better person.

We always went to church when I was growing up. But I did most of my growth in college at Alabama. I had a really good FCA (Fellowship of Christian Athletes) leader. Being around peers and people who had similar successes and similar failures, it's good to be around fellow Christians who hold each other accountable. I learned it's not about going to a specific church every Sunday or paying your dues. It's about having a personal relationship with Christ. That sort of gets lost in the shuffle sometimes. It's most important to spend quality time alone with Christ.

Jimmy Nelson

POSITION	Pitcher
HEIGHT	6 foot 6
WEIGHT	250 lbs
BATS	Right
THROWS	Right
NUMBER	52
BORN	June 5, 1989, in Klamath Falls, Oregon
HIGH SCHOOL	Niceville (Niceville, Florida)
COLLEGE	Alabama
DRAFTED	By Milwaukee Brewers in 2nd round of the 2010 amateur draft
HONORS	2014 Brewers Minor League Pitcher of the Year
TEAMS	Milwaukee Brewers (2013–)

Nelson's father played football at Florida, and his mother played basketball at Florida State.

A two-sport star in high school, Jimmy Nelson played baseball at college football powerhouse Alabama and quickly became one of Milwaukee's top prospects after he was drafted. Nelson pitched well in 2015, winning 11 games.

CAREER STATS

PITCHING				
Games	GS	W	L	CG
80	75	21	38	0
SHO	SV	ERA	IP	K
0	0	4.38	436	353

HECTOR NERIS

"When you pass through the waters, I will be with you; and when you pass through the rivers, they will not sweep over you. When you walk through the fire, you will not be burned; the flames will not set you ablaze."

ISAIAH 43:2

I like this verse because it's a daily reminder that whenever we go through hard times, we won't be defeated. We won't be burned. God is always with us, and He's always looking out for us. You just have to trust and believe in Him and have a relationship with Him. Whenever I go through rough times on the mound or off the field, I read the Bible and ask God for His help. He sent His Son, Jesus, to this world to suffer and die for our sins, so the least we can do is turn to Him and do what will make Him happy.

I've been a Christian all my life. When I was one year old, my mom became a Christian, so I was blessed to grow up in the faith with my mother, my sister, and my grandmother. I've always relied on God and had faith in Him, and He has guided me through my life.

Hector Neris

POSITION Pitcher

HEIGHT 6 foot 2

WEIGHT 215 lbs

BATS Right

THROWS Right

NUMBER 50

BORN June 14, 1989, in Villa Altagracia, San Cristobal, Dominican Republic

SIGNED By Philadelphia Phillies as amateur free agent in 2010

TEAMS Philadelphia Phillies (2014–)

Neris had a 13-game scoreless streak in 2016, in which he struck out 20 batters in 13.2 innings.

Hector Neris was one of Philadelphia's most consistent relievers in 2016, showing potential to be a setup man or closer of the future. Neris had a 2.58 ERA and struck out 102 batters in only 80.1 innings.

CAREER STATS

PITCHING				
Games	GS	W	L	CG
112	0	7	6	0
SHO	SV	ERA	IP	K
0	2	2.96	121.2	144

AARON NOLA

A person's steps are directed by the Lord.
How then can anyone understand their own way?

PROVERBS 20:24

I put this verse to use in baseball because it's easy for us when things are going bad to plan and think our way through what might happen. For me, this verse makes me think, *Why try to make our own plan? Why try to do it ourselves if God already has a plan for us?*

My family has been going to church since I was a little kid. They brought me up in the church, and I went to Catholic schools. But I feel that being a baseball player has brought me closer to God because there are many struggles I've never faced before and a lot of challenges I never faced before, especially at this level. It's the first time I have faced these kinds of challenges, and it's something I want to get through with the Lord. That's made me rely on Him a lot more. You have to do that because He's always with us. We're not alone, so why not turn to Him every chance we get?

The Bible has all the answers. It tells you how to live. Every part of the Bible says different things. It's all about faith in the Lord and putting Him first. He's always with you. You're in this together. You're never alone. He's everything you need.

Aaron Nola

POSITION Pitcher

HEIGHT 6 foot 2

WEIGHT 195 lbs

BATS Right

THROWS Right

NUMBER 27

BORN June 4, 1993, in Baton Rouge, Louisiana

HIGH SCHOOL Catholic HS, (Baton Rouge, Louisiana)

COLLEGE Louisiana State

DRAFTED By Philadelphia Phillies in 1st round of the 2014 amateur draft

HONORS Two-time SEC Pitcher of the Year

TEAMS Philadelphia Phillies (2015–)

Nola's brother, Austin Nola, is a catcher in the Miami Marlins' minor league system.

Aaron Nola quickly rose through Philadelphia's minor-league system and made his debut with the Phillies one year after he was drafted, becoming the first player drafted by the team to reach the major leagues the next season since 1989. Nola had an impressive rookie campaign, going 6-2.

CAREER STATS

PITCHING				
Games	GS	W	L	CG
33	33	12	11	0
SHO	SV	ERA	IP	K
0	0	4.29	188.2	189

BRETT OBERHOLTZER

Jesus talks a lot about love. When I was growing up, my parents would take me to church, and a lot of time I didn't understand what was going on. I didn't understand the context behind the Bible. As I grew older, I fell off the path a little bit. I got lost, so I went back to the way I was raised and started reading the Bible for the second time. I went through some of the chapters and decoded it for myself to understand what Jesus did. He died for our sins and opened up love for us to pass to one another. We shouldn't revert to hate, sin, jealousy, and all those things because they bring you down to a realm that's not familiar to us. As human beings, we're meant to love one another, and it's hard sometimes to do so. But you have to forgive and pray for others that might do harm to you and others.

Once I started following certain passages in the Bible, taking them to heart, and living my life like that, I started seeing a greater difference in my life and the people around me. I think that's our purpose on earth—to inspire, help, and love one another. That's our calling. It's hard in the world we live in right now because our society is all about who can get to the top first. All men are created equal, but society wrongly teaches us some are better than others. You have to always carry love in your heart, and it'll bring out the best in you.

Brett Oberholtzer

POSITION Pitcher

HEIGHT 6 foot 1

WEIGHT 225 lbs

BATS Left

THROWS Left

NUMBER 38

BORN July 1, 1989, in Christiana, Delaware

HIGH SCHOOL William Penn (New Castle, Delaware)

COLLEGE Seminole Community College

DRAFTED By Atlanta Braves in 8th round of 2008 amateur draft

HONORS 2013 Astros Pitcher of the Year by the Houston chapter of the Baseball Writers Association of America

TEAMS Houston Astros (2013–15); Philadelphia Phillies (2016); Los Angeles Angels (2016–)

Oberholtzer was ejected from a game for throwing inside to Alex Rodriguez in June 2015.

Brett Oberholtzer had an outstanding rookie season for the Astros in 2013, posting a 2.24 ERA and going 4-5 with two complete games and one shutout in 10 starts. He battled inconsistency over the next two seasons, was traded to Philadelphia, and moved to the bullpen.

CAREER STATS

PITCHING				
Games	GS	W	L	CG
82	44	14	23	2
SHO	SV	ERA	IP	K
2	1	4.36	324	220

JIMMY PAREDES

I keep my eyes always on the LORD.
With him at my right hand, I will not be shaken.

PSALM 16:8

Sometimes when you're trying to fall asleep or you're alone, you feel very lonely and that no one is with you, but this psalm tells you that God is always with you and He will keep you protected at all times.

When I was a kid, I was always interested in the Word of God. I always believed in God, and I knew He is always watching over us. I started reading the Bible more a few years ago, and I became an even bigger believer.

We tend to not give time to God, but we always should make time for Him and put all our trust in Him. There is a time for everything, and we should never forget that God is the one who provides for us. He has given us everything we have.

You can learn a lot from the Bible. Reading the Bible has helped me change for the better as a person in many aspects. Even things that you think you can't change about yourself, when you read the Bible, you feel like God is talking to you directly, and you make those changes and become even better.

Jimmy Paredes

POSITION Outfielder, infielder

HEIGHT 6 foot 3

WEIGHT 200 lbs

BATS Both

THROWS Right

NUMBER 41

BORN November 25, 1988, in Bajos de Haina, San Cristobal, Dominican Republic

SIGNED By New York Yankees as amateur free agent in 2006

HONORS 2012 Double-A All-Star, 2013 Triple-A All-Star

TEAMS Houston Astros (2011–13); Kansas City Royals (2014); Baltimore Orioles (2014–15); Toronto Blue Jays (2016); Philadelphia Phillies (2016–)

Paredes walked in his only postseason plate appearance with Baltimore in 2014.

Jimmy Paredes had his best season in 2015 when he played more than he did in any other season. Paredes batted .275 with 29 extra-base hits and 42 RBIs for the Orioles. He was claimed off waivers by Toronto and played for the Blue Jays and Phillies in 2016.

CAREER STATS

BATTING			
Games	AVG	OBP	SLG
332	.251	.286	.369
Hits	HR	RBI	SB
239	20	100	19

ANDY PETTITTE

But he gives us more grace. That is why Scripture says:
"God opposes the proud but shows favor to the humble."

JAMES 4:6

I consider this my life verse because I know God wants us all to be humble and show grace to others. Jesus Christ is the center of my life and my family's life, and our faith dictates everything we do. We are definitely not perfect, but we try to always put Christ first in every area of our lives.

We're living our lives right now on earth for treasures that I think that we will have in heaven, and I'm excited for the day I'm able to spend eternity with Jesus.

The most important thing in my life is my relationship with the Lord, trying to spread the Word of Jesus Christ, and trying to get people to get saved. The day I was saved, something changed in me. I knew that I was going to spend eternity in heaven with Him. But you have to accept Him. He has to be living inside of you. If you don't know Him, just ask Him to come into your heart and accept Him. It's not going to solve all your problems in the world, but it makes life a lot better.

Andy Pettitte

POSITION Pitcher

HEIGHT 6 foot 5

WEIGHT 235 lbs

BATS Left

THROWS Left

NUMBER 46

BORN June 15, 1972, in Baton Rouge, Louisiana

HIGH SCHOOL Deer Park (Deer Park, Texas)

COLLEGE San Jacinto College

DRAFTED By New York Yankees in 2nd round of 1990 amateur draft

HONORS Three-time American League All-Star, 2001 American League championship series Most Valuable Player

TEAMS New York Yankees (1995–2003); Houston Astros (2004–06); New York Yankees (2007–10, 2012–13)

Pettitte is tied with Whitey Ford for most starts in Yankees franchise history with 438.

Andy Pettitte was one of the top left-handed pitchers in the majors for almost two decades and helped the Yankees win five World Series championships during two separate stints in New York.

CAREER STATS

PITCHING				
Games	GS	W	L	CG
531	521	256	153	26
SHO	SV	ERA	IP	K
4	0	3.85	3,316	2,448

DAVID PHELPS

In this game, there are a lot of ups and downs, and for a lot of people, there are more downs than ups. We play a game of failure. It's really easy to get discouraged and ride that wave. This verse talks about not being discouraged, staying strong, and the Lord will be your guide. As athletes, we are put here not just to play baseball. We're given these gifts to glorify God, and we're given this pedestal to be that light. You sometimes get so caught up in baseball and your struggles and you forget what your real purpose is in life. We have to always remember there is a bigger purpose and understand baseball isn't the way you define yourself. There's a way to define ourselves, and it's through the Lord and our walk with Him. That's way more important than what we do on the field.

People see us playing this game because we are incredibly talented, but where does all that talent come from? It comes from God. I hope they realize that without God, all of this isn't possible. He gave us this talent and this platform to glorify Him.

David Phelps

POSITION	Pitcher
HEIGHT	6 foot 2
WEIGHT	200 lbs
BATS	Right
THROWS	Right
NUMBER	35
BORN	October 9, 1986, in St. Louis, Missouri
HIGH SCHOOL	Hazelwood (Florissant, Missouri)
COLLEGE	Notre Dame
DRAFTED	By New York Yankees in 14th round of 2008 amateur draft
HONORS	Yankees minor league "Pitcher of the Year" in 2010
TEAMS	New York Yankees (2012–2014); Miami Marlins (2015–)

David Phelps has developed into a reliable reliever after bouncing back and forth between the starting rotation and the bullpen over his first several seasons. Phelps posted a 2.28 ERA and appeared in a career high 64 games in 2016.

CAREER STATS

PITCHING				
Games	GS	W	L	CG
174	64	26	28	0
SHO	SV	ERA	IP	K
1	5	3.94	498	458

ALBERT PUJOLS

Whoever is kind to the poor lends to the LORD,
and he will reward them for what they have done.

PROVERBS 19:17

There's more to life than the game of baseball. My wife is the one who took me to church, and she explained to me the difference between eternal life and hell. I told her I wanted to go to heaven, and the next week I dedicated my life to the Lord. That was the turning point in my life because it felt as if my life was changing and transforming. It was amazing. It was the best decision I ever made. In 2000, after two years as a Christian, I realized it wasn't just a religion; it was about having a personal relationship with Jesus. And that's when I realized it wasn't about me anymore; it was about Him, and it was about serving others and sharing this great career that God gave me.

God gave me the platform to play baseball, but my job is to win souls for Jesus Christ. It's about Christ, about serving Him on the field and off the field. It's about me touching and changing lives. As believers, our rewards aren't here on earth. Our rewards are in heaven. I give Him all the credit for what I have done. I don't want people to remember me as a baseball player. Off the field is more important than what I do on the field.

Albert Pujols

POSITION First baseman

HEIGHT 6 foot 3

WEIGHT 240 lbs

BATS Right

THROWS Right

NUMBER 5

BORN January 16, 1980, in Santo Domingo, Distrito Nacional, Dominican Republic

HIGH SCHOOL Fort Osage (Independence, Missouri)

COLLEGE Maple Woods Community College

DRAFTED By St. Louis Cardinals in 13th round of the 1999 amateur draft

HONORS Ten-time All-Star, 2001 National League Rookie of the Year, three-time National League Most Valuable Player, two-time National League Gold Glove Award winner

TEAMS St. Louis Cardinals (2001–11); Los Angeles Angels (2012–)

SEVENTH INNING STRETCH

Pujols has averaged just 70 strikeouts per season and has more career walks than strikeouts.

Albert Pujols has been one of the best sluggers in the major leagues for more than a decade. He combines raw power with the ability to hit for a high average. Pujols has hit at least 40 homers in a season seven times, and he's driven in 100 or more runs 13 times. Pujols is a certain first-ballot Hall of Famer.

CAREER STATS

BATTING			
Games	AVG	OBP	SLG
2,426	.309	.392	.573
Hits	HR	RBI	SB
2,825	591	1,817	107

NEIL RAMIREZ

Paul is such an amazing speaker, and he says we were dead in our trespasses and sins. We weren't spiritually hanging on. We weren't spiritually on our last breath. We were dead. The only thing that could save us was the resurrection. And this passage starts: "But God." I think about how God intervened right there where we were dead. We needed God in that moment to save us, and that's exactly what He did. He sent His perfect and spotless Son because of His great love for us to save us. That was all His grace. There were no works that we could do to get to that place, because we deserved death.

But God loved us so much, He sent His one and only Son to save us and raise us up with Him and seat us with Him in heavenly places through Christ's resurrection and through the perfect life He lived and how He willingly sacrificed Himself on the cross on our behalf. It's an amazing verse to see the state of where we were and what God did on our behalf because He loved us so much.

I didn't grow up in the church. I was kind of going by what this world told me was okay. I always thought of myself as a good person, but the more I get into scripture now and see how this world works, I understand why Paul tells us we are all inherently evil; sin is in our nature. I was in the minor leagues in 2010, and I was blessed to have a roommate, Robbie Ross, who encouraged me to go to chapel, and the more I went, the more I felt this tug at my heart. I got to the point where this was real and I believed that Jesus is the only one who can save me. I gave myself to Christ at the end of that year.

Neil Ramirez

POSITION Pitcher

HEIGHT 6 foot 4

WEIGHT 215 lbs

BATS Right

THROWS Right

NUMBER 50

BORN May 25, 1989, in Virginia Beach, Virginia

HIGH SCHOOL Kempsville (Virginia Beach, Virginia)

DRAFTED By Texas Rangers in 1st round (44th overall) of 2007 amateur draft

HONORS Rangers Minor League Pitcher of the Month (April 2011)

TEAMS Chicago Cubs (2014–16); Milwaukee Brewers (2016); Minnesota Twins (2016–)

Ramirez spent his honeymoon with wife, Tiffany, helping children at an orphanage in Haiti.

Neil Ramirez broke into the majors in 2014 and had an outstanding season. He posted a 1.44 ERA in 50 appearances as a reliever for the Cubs. Ramirez began the 2016 season in Chicago and ended it in Minnesota with a stop in Milwaukee along the way.

CAREER STATS

PITCHING				
Games	GS	W	L	CG
87	0	4	3	0
SHO	SV	ERA	IP	K
0	3	3.09	81.2	92

WILSON RAMOS

I can do all this through him who gives me strength.

PHILIPPIANS 4:13

This is a very significant verse to me because it has given me a lot of strength over the past few years, especially the time when I was kidnapped in Venezuela and held captive for fifty-five hours. I didn't know if I was going to get out of it alive. This verse helped me get through that situation. That's why I have it tattooed on my arm, along with the date I was rescued (11-11-11) because it helps me remember Christ gave me the strength to endure.

I grew up in a Christian environment. My mom and my grandparents on my dad's side were Christians, so I've been around Christianity my whole life. It's how I was raised. I try to participate and attend baseball chapel every Sunday during the season, and I definitely go when they offer chapel in Spanish. It enables me to understand it a lot better. I enjoy going because it relaxes me and helps me keep focused on what's important.

Wilson Ramos

POSITION Catcher

HEIGHT 6 foot 1

WEIGHT 255 lbs

BATS Right

THROWS Right

NUMBER 40

BORN August 10, 1987 in Valencia, Carabobo, Venezuela

HIGH SCHOOL U. E. Santa Ines (Venezuela)

SIGNED By Minnesota Twins as amateur free agent in 2004

HONORS 2016 All-Star

TEAMS Minnesota Twins (2010), Washington Nationals (2010–)

Ramos was the first Twins player since Hall of Famer Kirby Puckett in 1984 to collect four hits in a major league debut, and the only catcher in modern history (since 1900) to collect four hits in his debut.

An excellent defensive catcher, Wilson Ramos developed into one of the best hitters at his position. He had his best season in 2016, setting career highs in batting average (.307), home runs (22), and runs batted in (80). His season was cut short after he tore the anterior cruciate ligament in his right knee for the second time in his career.

CAREER STATS

BATTING			
Games	AVG	OBP	SLG
585	.269	.313	.430
Hits	HR	RBI	SB
574	83	321	20

J. T. REALMUTO

This verse speaks to me because I've been taught my whole life through Jesus Christ and my family to stay humble in whatever you do, so it has stuck with me from the beginning. It's a key point to my character and how I go about my life.

It's tough to be humble in the industry we're in and the limelight we're put in, but it's extremely important to be humble and understand that all of this is just a small part of what we do. A lot of people don't see that. We need to stay humble, stay low-key, and not buy into all the fame and the things of this world. It's a struggle for many people, and it's something I work really hard to avoid.

Reading the Bible every day and getting into the Word fulfills things throughout your body and your soul that you can't get anywhere else. It just gives you a sense of peace that you can't find anywhere else.

J. T. Realmuto

POSITION Catcher

HEIGHT 6 foot 1

WEIGHT 210 lbs

BATS Right

THROWS Right

NUMBER 11

BORN March 18, 1991, in Del City, Oklahoma

HIGH SCHOOL Carl Albert (Midwest City, Oklahoma)

DRAFTED By Miami Marlins in 3rd round of 2010 amateur draft

HONORS 2015 Rookie of the Year by South Florida chapter of the Baseball

TEAMS Miami Marlins (2015–)

On September 8, 2015, Realmuto became the first catcher with an inside-the-park homer and another homer in the same game since Hall of Famer Gary Carter did it in 1980.

A standout athlete, J. T. Realmuto passed up a scholarship to Oklahoma State to sign with the Marlins and convert from shortstop to catcher. He's quickly become one of the top hitting catchers in the majors and batted .303 in 2016.

CAREER STATS

BATTING			
Games	AVG	OBP	SLG
274	.281	.317	.416
Hits	HR	RBI	SB
275	21	104	20

BEN REVERE

Whoever dwells in the shelter of the Most High will rest in the shadow of the Almighty. I will say of the LORD, "He is my refuge and my fortress, my God, in whom I trust."

PSALM 91:1–2

I grew up in a Christian family. My grandfather was a preacher, so I used to go to his services when I was growing up in Georgia. My grandma would spank me if I fell asleep in church. My dad was always there for us, and he taught me the Bible as a young kid. My mom always sends me Bible verses and prayers. It helped me grow up to become a mature person and changed my mindset. My grandfather really got my mind geared on Psalm 91. Every day, we may go through some trouble in our lives, especially in the game of baseball.

When I read this passage, it's definitely heartfelt, and you realize whatever you may be going through, whatever temptations are in your life, God is saying to you: *"Don't give up on me, and I'll help you overcome anything and have a long life of salvation."* Reading this passage makes me realize that God has a better plan for me. I like to read it especially if something isn't going well because it's a constant reminder that the Big Man upstairs is always by your side no matter what.

You see so many athletes waste their talent because their egos become so big and they think they can handle everything on their own, but no matter what gifts and blessings God gave you, He could take it away very quickly.

Ben Revere

POSITION	Outfielder
HEIGHT	5 foot 9
WEIGHT	175 lbs
BATS	Left
THROWS	Right
NUMBER	9
BORN	May 3, 1988, in Atlanta, Georgia
HIGH SCHOOL	Lexington Catholic (Lexington, Kentucky)
DRAFTED	By Minnesota Twins in 1st round of the 2007 amateur draft
HONORS	American League Rookie of the Month (June 2011)
TEAMS	Minnesota Twins (2010–12); Philadelphia Phillies (2013–15); Toronto Blue Jays (2015); Washington Nationals (2016)

It took 1,466 career at-bats before Revere hit his first home run in 2014.

Ben Revere established himself as one of the top singles hitters in the major leagues between 2012–15 when he batted over .300 three straight seasons. He stole 49 bases for the Phillies in 2014 when he led the National League with 184 hits.

CAREER STATS

BATTING			
Games	AVG	OBP	SLG
748	.285	.320	.342
Hits	HR	RBI	SB
812	6	178	190

MARIANO RIVERA

Jesus looked at them and said, "With man this is impossible, but with God all things are possible."

MATTHEW 19:26

My career, all of my success was a gift from the Lord. He allowed me to get results way beyond my physical abilities. I threw one pitch, yet I was successful as a closer for the New York Yankees for all those years with that one pitch. Why? Because of the Lord. I accomplished everything through the Lord and His strength, not my strength. His love, His mercy, and His strength allowed me to do everything I did on the field. He used me for His own purposes so that I would help spread the good news about Jesus. And if He used me, He could use anybody. You have to line up with His heart, and when you face adversity, trust in the Lord and have faith in the Lord because you can't do it on your own. You can only do it by His power.

I know my job is to glorify the Lord and praise His name and lead others to seek Him and want to experience His grace and peace and mercy.

I don't want people to recognize me for my accomplishments in baseball. I want them to know me for who I am as a Christian.

Mariano Rivera

POSITION	Pitcher
HEIGHT	6 foot 2
WEIGHT	195 lbs
BATS	Right
THROWS	Right
NUMBER	42
BORN	November 29, 1969, in Panama City, Panama
HIGH SCHOOL	La Chorrea (Panama City, Panama)
SIGNED	By New York Yankees as amateur free agent in 1990
HONORS	13-time All-Star, 1999 World Series Most Valuable Player, five-time Rolaids Relief Man of the Year, 2013 American League Comeback Player of the Year
TEAMS	New York Yankees (1995–2013)

Rivera had 44 saves at 43 years old in his final season.

Mariano Rivera was the most dominant closer in major league history. He holds the all-time record for most saves with 652 and saved 42 games in the postseason, helping the Yankees win five World Series championships. Rivera had a 0.70 ERA in 96 postseason games.

CAREER STATS

PITCHING				
Games	GS	W	L	CG
1,115	10	82	60	0
SHO	SV	ERA	IP	K
0	652	2.21	1,283.2	1,173

RENE RIVERA

I can do all this through him who gives me strength.

PHILIPPIANS 4:13

I've been in difficult situations in my life and in my career. I've been at the top and at the bottom. But this verse helps me overcome all the difficult moments. When I was down in my career, I was a big believer in putting Christ first in my life, and now I am here.

God knows what's best for your life. He already has your life written. So just believe in Him and let Him do His job, and everything will work out right. Life has tough moments, but if you follow and believe God, He knows what's best for you, and your life will be much better.

I grew up going to church in Puerto Rico. It was right near my house. Since the day I walked into church, I fell in love with God. I fell in love with the people there. Every time I go to church, I see how life is so much different, and how much better it is if you follow God.

Rene Rivera

POSITION	Catcher
HEIGHT	5 foot 10
WEIGHT	215 lbs
BATS	Right
THROWS	Right
NUMBER	44
BORN	July 31, 1983, in Bayamon, Puerto Rico
HIGH SCHOOL	Papa Juan (Bayamon, Puerto Rico)
DRAFTED	By Seattle Mariners in 2nd round of the 2001 amateur draft
HONORS	2013 Triple-A All-Star
TEAMS	Seattle Marines (2004–06); Minnesota Twins (2011); San Diego Padres (2013–14); Tampa Bay Rays (2015); New York Mets (2016–)

Rivera started for the Mets in the 2016 wild-card playoff game, was 1 for 3 at the plate, and threw out a base runner.

Rene Rivera broke into the majors in 2004 and played sparingly over three seasons. He spent four full seasons in the minors before returning to the majors and establishing himself as a solid backup catcher with the Padres, Rays, and Mets over the past three seasons.

CAREER STATS

BATTING			
Games	AVG	OBP	SLG
399	.213	.264	.332
Hits	HR	RBI	SB
234	26	118	1

JOHN SMOLTZ

"I am the vine; you are the branches. If you remain in me and I in you, you will bear much fruit; apart from me you can do nothing."

JOHN 15:5

I went to church, went to Bible study, and tried to do good and honor my family and God, but I didn't understand the importance of having that relationship with Christ. When I accepted Jesus as my Savior in 1995, I finally understood that being saved is not just a prayer; it's a surrender. It's a heartfelt contract. It's an opportunity to know that everything that He's given us in the Bible is for our benefit.

So when I gave my life over to Him and gave Him that backpack of junk I was carrying, it didn't make life easier. It didn't make baseball easier. But the peace that transcends all understanding became the essence of my life as a walking Christian professing my faith. I was so fortunate through arm injuries, through some of the toughest times, He brought me to my knees, and that's where I needed to ask Him for guidance.

I encourage people to read the Bible to see the principles He's given us that have withstood the test of time and give us the answers on what it's like to live a grace-filled life.

John Smoltz

POSITION	Pitcher
HEIGHT	6 foot 3
WEIGHT	210 lbs
BATS	Right
THROWS	Right
NUMBER	29
BORN	May 15, 1967, in Detroit, Michigan
HIGH SCHOOL	Waverly (Lansing, Michigan)
DRAFTED	By Detroit Tigers in the 22nd round of the 1985 amateur draft
HONORS	Inducted into the Hall of Fame in 2015; eight-time National League All-Star; 1996 National League Cy Young Award winner; 1992 National League championship series Most Valuable Player; 2002 National League Rolaids Relief Award winner
TEAMS	Atlanta Braves (1988–2008); Boston Red Sox (2009); St. Louis Cardinals (2009)

Smoltz was in the minor leagues when the Tigers traded him to Atlanta for pitcher Doyle Alexander in one of baseball's most lopsided deals.

John Smoltz was one of the best big-game pitchers in major league history. He was 15-4 with a 2.67 ERA in the postseason and helped the Braves win the World Series in 1995. Smoltz is the only player in major league history with at least 200 wins and 150 saves. He was part of a rotation that featured future Hall of Famers Greg Maddux and Tom Glavine. His number is retired by the Braves.

CAREER STATS

PITCHING				
Games	GS	W	L	CG
723	481	213	155	53
SHO	SV	ERA	IP	K
16	154	3.33	3,473	3,084

BRANDON SNYDER

*"Therefore do not worry about tomorrow,
for tomorrow will worry about itself.
Each day has enough trouble of its own."*

MATTHEW 6:34

In baseball, you often worry about tomorrow, how well you'll play, where you're going to be. This game moves you all around. Early in my career, it was a source of anxiety because you start looking behind you and thinking about what you have to do to be here tomorrow, to be a better player. If you realize that you can give it to God, not worry about tomorrow, and let Him lead you, that takes a lot of anxiety away and lets you be yourself. I have this verse tattooed on my arm, and I continue to remind myself to think about today and not worry about tomorrow.

One of our biggest problems in society is people putting their Bibles away. If you can get more into the Word and start understanding who God is, you won't be afraid of God, and you'll understand the love and compassion He has for us. That's the part people get skewed sometimes.

If you look at Christian athletes, we're fortunate to be considered heroes to kids, but we understand everything we are and all the abilities we've been given come from Christ. To be where we are is our platform to express our love for Christ and thankfulness for all we've been given. Sometimes that's put on the back burner, and it needs to be up front.

Brandon Snyder

POSITION First baseman, third baseman

HEIGHT 6 foot 2

WEIGHT 225 lbs

BATS Right

THROWS Right

NUMBER 19

BORN June 15, 1949, in Riverside, California

HIGH SCHOOL Westfield HS (Chantilly, Virginia)

DRAFTED By Baltimore Orioles in 1st round (13th overall) of the 2005 amateur draft

HONORS *Washington Post*'s 2005 High School Player of the Year

TEAMS Baltimore Orioles (2010–11); Texas Rangers (2012); Boston Red Sox (2013); Atlanta Braves (2016–)

Brandon Snyder is the son of former major league pitcher, Brian Snyder.

Brandon Snyder hit his first major league home run against Toronto Blue Jays starter Ricky Romero at the Rogers Centre in May 2012, seven years after he was a first-round draft pick. Snyder played 27 games for the Red Sox during their World Series title run in 2013.

CAREER STATS

BATTING			
Games	AVG	OBP	SLG
120	.242	.279	.459
Hits	HR	RBI	SB
47	9	29	0

JOAKIM SORIA

The LORD is my shepherd, I lack nothing.

PSALM 23:1 (EMPHASIS ADDED)

I like this verse because it says if we honor Him, seek Him, and follow Him, He has our back in everything, and He's going to protect us. I want Jesus to be my shepherd, and He is going to be our shepherd.

When I became a Christian in 2012, I felt I started to develop a relationship with God. Before it was more like a code. Yes, I grew up Catholic, but I did whatever I wanted. When I came to God, I started reading the Bible. It opened my eyes, and I started to see things differently. My relationship with my wife, my kids, my parents—with everybody—became different. My behavior became different, and it changed my life.

I encourage children to read the Bible so they can have their own knowledge about the scriptures. Life is different than what the world shows us. Don't follow the world. Seek Him and you'll find what is really important in your life.

Joakim Soria

POSITION	Pitcher
HEIGHT	6 foot 3
WEIGHT	200 lbs
BATS	Right
THROWS	Right
NUMBER	48
BORN	May 18, 1984, in Monclova, Coahuila, Mexico
SIGNED	By Kansas City Royals as amateur free agent in 2015
HONORS	Two-time All-Star, one-time Gold Glove Award winner
TEAMS	Kansas City Royals (2006–12, 2015–); Texas Rangers (2012–13); Detroit Tigers (2014-15); Pittsburgh Pirates (2015)

Soria represented Mexico in the 2009 World Baseball Classic, recording a pair of scoreless appearances.

A two-time All-Star closer, Joakim Soria averaged 36 saves per season over a four-year span with the Royals from 2008–11. He played for three other teams and earned at least one save with each before returning to Kansas City in 2016.

CAREER STATS

PITCHING				
Games	GS	W	L	CG
514	0	24	28	0
SHO	SV	ERA	IP	K
0	203	2.76	517.2	549

DANIEL STUMPF

Let the fields be jubilant, and everything in them;
let all the trees of the forest sing for joy.

PSALM 96:12

This verse is stitched into my glove, and it's one of my favorite ones because it fits into playing baseball. I grew up going to church because my family went. I was involved in kid groups and youth camps, and when I got to college, I helped with leading small groups in church. My brother is a youth pastor.

When I was twelve years old, I went to a camp and I asked Christ into my life. I was always around Christianity, and going to church was a part of my life. But at a young age, it's hard to understand things. Nowadays, there's a lot of Bibles out there that are translated so it's easier to understand .

Being a bold Christian is not the norm, and people are shying away from it. But you can't avoid going out and trying to reach people and talk to them about God because you're scared of what the world might think of you. There's so much going on in this world right now, and we need to put Christ back in the world.

Daniel Stumpf

POSITION	Pitcher
HEIGHT	6 foot 2
WEIGHT	200 lbs
BATS	Left
THROWS	Left
NUMBER	53
BORN	January 4, 1991, in Humble, Texas
HIGH SCHOOL	Atascocita (Humble, Texas)
COLLEGE	San Jacinto College
DRAFTED	By Kansas City Royals in 9th round of 2012 amateur draft
HONORS	2013 Single-A All-Star
TEAMS	Philadelphia Phillies (2016)

SEVENTH INNING STRETCH

Stumpf didn't allow a run in five of his seven games with the Phillies.

Daniel Stumpf began the 2016 season with the Phillies after he was selected in the Rule 5 draft. Stumpf appeared in seven games before he was returned to the Royals. He had a 2.14 ERA in 14 appearances for Kansas City's Double-A affiliate.

CAREER STATS

PITCHING

Games	GS	W	L	CG
7	0	0	0	0

SHO	SV	ERA	IP	K
0	0	10.80	5	2

MARK TEIXEIRA

For the Scripture says, "Whoever believes in him will not be disappointed."

ROMANS 10:11 WEB

Baseball is a game of failure. If you put all your dreams and hopes and aspirations in what you're doing on the field, you will be disappointed every day. You're always going to be let down. But when you have God in your life and you follow Christ, you're never going to be let down. God has never disappointed us. Whether it's failure or success, I know I have to rely on His will.

When my son was born, I finally realized how selfish I had been for twenty-five years, and everything was put into perspective. The love God has for me is the same unconditional love I have for my son.

So I put Christ first in my life—not baseball. I put my family behind Him, and I put baseball down the line. Obviously, I want to succeed. But the more important thing is being a Christian and being in the kingdom of heaven.

I'm nothing without God, and it doesn't matter who you are, if you think you can live life on your own without God, you'll be disappointed a lot. No matter what you're doing, you need to be doing it to glorify God.

Mark Teixeira

POSITION	First baseman
HEIGHT	6 foot 3
WEIGHT	225 lbs
BATS	Both
THROWS	Right
NUMBER	25
BORN	April 11, 1980, in Annapolis, Maryland
HIGH SCHOOL	Mount St. Joseph's (Baltimore, Maryland)
COLLEGE	Georgia Institute of Technology
DRAFTED	By Texas Rangers in 1st round (5th overall) of the 2001 amateur draft
HONORS	Three-time All-Star, five-time Gold Glove Award winner, three-time Silver Slugger Award winner
TEAMS	Texas Rangers (2003–07); Atlanta Braves (2007–08); Los Angeles Angels (2008); New York Yankees (2009–16)

Teixeira holds the all-time major league record for most games with a home run from both sides of the plate, with 14.

Mark Teixeira was an excellent defensive first baseman and one of the best all-around switch hitters in major league history. He ranks fifth in career home runs with 409. Teixeira finished second in voting for American League Most Valuable Player in 2009 and helped the Yankees win the World Series.

CAREER STATS

BATTING			
Games	AVG	OBP	SLG
1,862	.268	.360	.509
Hits	HR	RBI	SB
1,862	409	1,298	26

ADAM WAINWRIGHT

However, I consider my life worth nothing to me; my only aim is to finish the race and complete the task the Lord Jesus has given me—the task of testifying to the good news of God's grace.

ACTS 20:24

I grew up in southeast Georgia, the Bible Belt. Everyone went to church. I was in church every Sunday, but there were a lot of things I didn't like or understand about church. I knew the Bible, I knew the prayers, but I didn't have a relationship with Christ. I even doubted if there was a God. One year I went to spring training, and one of my roommates, Blaine Boyer, was a Christian and he was living it.

There was something different about him. He had that glow in his eye, and I wanted it. He encouraged me to go to a Pro Athletes Outreach meeting, and when I went there, I was just blown away by the way everyone loved each other and the passion in the room. It was the first time I heard the word *relationship* associated with Christianity. I came away a completely changed person. Christ changed my life dramatically. Now I try to see everything through His eyes. I know He has made me a better husband and parent. I know God is always watching, so I have accountability all the time.

Adam Wainwright

POSITION Pitcher

HEIGHT 6 foot 7

WEIGHT 235 lbs

BATS Right

THROWS Right

NUMBER 50

BORN August 30, 1981, in Brunswick, Georgia

HIGH SCHOOL Glynn Academy (Brunswick, Georgia)

DRAFTED By Atlanta Braves in 1st round (29th overall) of the 2000 amateur draft

HONORS Three-time National League All-Star, two-time Gold Glove Award winner

TEAMS St. Louis Cardinals (2005–)

Adam Wainwright began his career in the bullpen and became a closer during the 2006 postseason, helping the Cardinals win the World Series. He was converted to starter the following season and has been an ace on St. Louis' staff for a decade. He's won 20 games twice, 19 games twice, and four times finished in the top 3 in voting for NL Cy Young Award winner.

CAREER STATS

PITCHING				
Games	GS	W	L	CG
320	254	134	76	22
SHO	SV	ERA	IP	K
10	3	3.17	1,768.1	1,487

ADAM WARREN

"Have I not commanded you? Be strong and courageous. Do not be afraid; do not be discouraged, for the LORD your God will be with you wherever you go."

JOSHUA 1:9

I really like this verse because the world views Christians as weak and timid, but here is God saying the opposite. Be strong, be courageous. We're not called to be pushovers. This verse presents a pretty cool picture of the men we are supposed to be. He calls us to be the strong men that sometimes we get away from. This verse gives you confidence to do that.

The second part of the verse says God is always with you. It's just neat to have that reassurance that we can go out there and compete and be assertive and not feel like we're doing the wrong thing because that's what God taught us to be, to be strong and courageous.

You have to ask yourself the meaning of life, why you are living. If you search for answers, it always leads to the same place, and you'll find them in the Bible. When you realize who created you, and you realize your purpose and how much better it can be having eternity waiting for you in heaven, it makes life more enjoyable. People see Christianity as being bogged down by these rules, but there's more freedom than anything. If you truly want to live your life to the fullest, you have to find out what your purpose is.

Adam Warren

POSITION	Pitcher
HEIGHT	6 foot 1
WEIGHT	225 lbs
BATS	Right
THROWS	Right
NUMBER	43
BORN	August 25, 1987, in Birmingham, Alabama
HIGH SCHOOL	New Bern (New Bern, North Carolina)
COLLEGE	North Carolina
DRAFTED	By New York Yankees in 4th round of 2009 amateur draft
HONORS	ESPN's 2009 Academic All-America Third Team
TEAMS	New York Yankees (2012–2015, 2016–); Chicago Cubs (2016)

Warren was traded from the Yankees to the Cubs and back to the Yankees in a span of eight months.

Adam Warren made his major league debut on July 29, 2012, filling in for injured starter CC Sabathia. He moved to the bullpen the next season and had success as a reliever in 2014, posting a 2.97 ERA in 69 games.

CAREER STATS

PITCHING				
Games	GS	W	L	CG
205	21	20	19	0
SHO	SV	ERA	IP	K
0	5	3.63	354.2	297

BEN ZOBRIST

I have been crucified with Christ and I no longer live, but Christ lives in me. The life I now live in the body, I live by faith in the Son of God, who loved me and gave himself for me.

GALATIANS 2:20

This verse encompasses what I believe the good news is all about, the Gospel that God loved me even though I'm a sinner. He sent His Son to die on the cross for my sins, and He delivered me from my slavery to sin and ultimately, my death. I've been through times of struggle in my life, and that's the verse that I go back to and remind myself. Even when I'm struggling and I'm failing and I'm having a hard time looking in the mirror, the good news is that I've been replaced. I've been crucified with Christ. The old me is already gone. The new me is in Christ, and I'm safe, secure, and whole; and when God looks at me, He doesn't look at my failures. He doesn't see all my struggles and the inabilities that I have; He sees perfection through His Son, and that's my hope.

When you look at the Bible, don't look at it like a textbook or a chore. Look at it like it's God's love letter to us. He's speaking to you individually, and He's going to speak to you through the Holy Spirit and the Word. If we all look at it like that, we would understand it even more and we would cherish the words even more than we do. It's not a normal book; it's something to cherish and recognize this is your heavenly Father sharing your life with you.

Ben Zobrist

POSITION	Second baseman, outfielder
HEIGHT	6 foot 3
WEIGHT	210 lbs
BATS	Both
THROWS	Right
NUMBER	18
BORN	May 26, 1981, in Eureka, Illinois
HIGH SCHOOL	Eureka (Eureka, Illinois)
COLLEGE	Dallas Baptist University, Olivet Nazarene University
DRAFTED	By Houston Astros in 6th round of the 2004 amateur draft
HONORS	Three-time All-Star
TEAMS	Tampa Bay Rays (2006–14); Oakland A's (2015); Kansas City Royals (2015); Chicago Cubs (2016)

Ben Zobrist is married to Christian singer, Julianna Zobrist.

For a guy who wasn't recruited by colleges and wasn't thinking about a career in baseball after finishing high school, Ben Zobrist became one of the best versatile players in the league. He has started at seven different positions, played in three All-Star games, and three times finished in the top 20 in voting for Most Valuable Player.

CAREER STATS

BATTING			
Games	AVG	OBP	SLG
1,337	.266	.358	.433
Hits	HR	RBI	SB
1,287	145	643	111

ABOUT THE AUTHOR

Rob Maaddi has been a Philadelphia sports writer for The Associated Press since 2000. He's covered multiple Super Bowls, World Series, NBA Finals, Stanley Cup Finals, and numerous major sporting events throughout his career. Rob has coauthored three children's sports books, wrote a biography on Mike Schmidt, and wrote *Football Faith*. He is also a radio and television personality. A devoted Christian, Rob strives every day to make a difference and be a blessing. Rob is a missionary athlete with the Deacons Prison Ministry softball team. He visits inmates, shares his testimony, and preaches about Jesus Christ. Rob, his wife, Remy, and twin girls, Alexia and Melina, reside in South Jersey.

SCRIPTURE INDEX

ART CREDITS